Changing
Experiences
of Youth

Changing Experiences of Youth

EDITED BY
Daren Garratt,
Jeremy Roche and
Stanley Tucker

SAGE Publications
London • Thousand Oaks • New Delhi

in association with

The Open
University

First published in 1997
Reprinted 2000, 2002, 2003

The opinions expressed are not necessarily those of the
Course Team or of The Open University

SAGE Publications Ltd
6 Bonhill Street
London EC2A 4PU

SAGE Publications Inc
2455 Teller Road
Thousand Oaks, California 91320

SAGE Publications India Pvt Ltd
32, M-Block Market
Greater Kailash – I
New Delhi 110 048

British Library Cataloguing in Publication Data

A catalogue record for this book is available
from the British Library.

ISBN 0 7619 5374–4
ISBN 0 7619 5375–2 (pbk)

Library of Congress catalog card number 96–071241

Typeset by Mayhew Typesetting, Rhayader, Powys
Printed in Great Britain by Biddles Ltd, *www.biddles.co.uk*

Contents

Listed below are some specialist projects and organisations that have contributed to this volume:

ASC (Advice Advocacy and Representation Service for Children), Canterbury House, 1–3 Greengate, Salford, Manchester M3 7NN (0161-839 8442); **Crime Concern**, Signal Point, Station Road, Swindon SN1 1EE; **Cascade**, Keepers Lodge, Chelmsley Road, Chelmsley Wood, Solihull, West Midlands B37 7UA (0121-788 3436); **Dudley HIV and AIDS Support Group**, 34 Lower High Street, Stourbridge, West Midlands (01384 444300); **Homeless Project**, Wychbury Court, Queens Cross, Dudley; **London Connection**, 12 Adelaide Street, London WC2N 4HW (0171-321 0633); **NACRO** (National Association for the Care and Resettlement of Offenders), 169 Clapham Road, London SW9 0PU (0171-582 6500); **West Midlands Lesbian and Gay Switchboard**, PO Box 3626, Birmingham B5 4LG (0121-622 6589 7pm–10pm only).

Introduction

This book is concerned with the varied real-life experiences of young people and those who work with them. Most of the accounts presented here are first hand and our aim in compiling them is to highlight the many struggles and achievements of young people and workers.

In the UK today young people are seen as 'problematic': the young person is either a threat or a victim. The understandable 'respectable fears' surrounding young people's involvement in anti-social behaviour, violent crime, drug abuse and theft become, in the hands of the media and politicians, conclusive proof that 'fings ain't wot they used ta be' and that society is on the edge of collapse. The acts of individual young people become the 'problem of youth' and the myth of their degeneracy is perpetuated.

Here an attempt is made to challenge this myth by making available images of young people rarely seen in contemporary society. Young people are depicted as an oppressed group, openly discriminated against in local and national politics, and who have to struggle, mostly unnoticed, in order to overcome adult prejudices. The anthology is concerned that their voice be heard as well as that of the workers and organisations who encounter and support them in their search for autonomy and respect. We hope that this will inspire and promote better understanding of the lives of young people and improve working practices.

This anthology, like its companion volume *Youth in Society: Contemporary Theory, Policy and Practice* (edited by Jeremy Roche and Stanley Tucker), is presented as a positive contribution towards promoting the rights and responsibilities of young people in society. It is about the diversity of their lives and the issues which face them; it is concerned with what does happen, not what should happen. This essential aspect of the anthology is strengthened by the presentation of first-hand accounts of difficult issues like incest and anorexia, racism and other forms of violence by people who have survived and built upon these experiences.

The anthology captures three types of voice: those of young people themselves, those of the projects that work with young people, and those of individual workers. What these voices highlight is the desire and need to understand and accommodate the many different types of situations and dilemmas that young people find themselves in. These range from:

- Amir, who has had to adapt, since the age of 13, to life in a wheelchair (Chapter 4), to the young girls and women of Wolverhampton Wanderers Women's Football Team, who have had to overcome the prejudices of others in their struggle to be accepted as women in a 'man's' sport (Chapter 2), to the anger of young people faced with an abusive society (Chapter 10), abusive institutions (Chapter 33) or abusive relationships (Chapter 7).
- Organisations that assist young people in their own battle to beat crime (Chapter 19), to those that promote heightened awareness of safe sex (Chapter 9), to those that assist young people to make the transition from dependent to independent living (Chapter 14).
- Ann Cox's advice on how workers can detect and assist in beating eating disorders (Chapter 8), to Pat Patten's account of how black workers can empower black youth and tackle racism (Chapter 6), to the issues raised by setting up and running a group for young men on health matters (Chapter 28).

The voices of young people

The voices of young people form a powerful experiential thread throughout. The stories recounted are rich, varied and, in places, disturbing. They are used to tell positive tales of care and social responsibility. One aspect of the positive work that young people do in their own communities is featured here through the experiences of young carers (Chapter 11). There are an estimated 200,000 young people who have the task of caring for a sick or infirm member of their family. This responsibility which is accepted by the young carers is not made any easier by the attitudes of some of the professionals involved.

But for other young people life can be extremely difficult. In 'Exploring Homelessness' (Chapter 10) 'M.' tells us that it was domestic violence that led to her having to leave home, and that even though she had a social worker at the time, she was told that she didn't need help because she 'had got [her] head on [her] shoulders'. 'J.' also captures a lack of understanding on the part of the public by telling us how he was 'kicked, spat on because [he] was sleeping rough in the doorway'. He also graphically reports the attitudes of people to the homeless: 'people chuck all their litter over you. Generally they think you're a bit of "scum".'

Projects and empowering young people

The issue of empowering young people to actively voice their concerns and take a more proactive role in society is taken up throughout the volume. The chapter on bullying (Chapter 20) shows that young people, with adult support, can develop positive strategies in response to issues that affect them. This belief in the importance of young people's empowerment has already been put into practice by a number of organisations.

Andy Chaffer and his colleagues at West Midlands Lesbian and Gay Switchboard (Chapter 22), drawing on their own experiences of being gay teenagers, have found themselves better able to support young people.

Another group of volunteers doing positive youth work are the staff at an African-Caribbean Saturday school (Chapter 15) who are fighting racist educational assumptions by developing an alternative positive and stimulating environment. The intention is to 'give the pupils both the resources and the determination to succeed within a society in which they suffer from both racism and social class inequalities'.

But it is not only small, regional associations that are seen to be pioneering such positive interactive youth work. The work of Save the Children and its many projects are helping 'to provide a more positive and sensitive understanding of the mental health needs of disadvantaged young people' (Chapter 21), and NACRO's Youth Choices (Chapter 17) scheme is intended to give young people the relevant skills to help successfully ease the transition between dependent and independent living.

Workers talking

The success of projects and positive youth work ultimately boils down to the individual workers, and the last part of the anthology is dedicated to their perspectives and accounts. Here they talk about working with young people and the issues raised for them. One common theme is that those who work with young people need to think through how to enable the young person they are working with to recognise and overcome their problems and dilemmas for themselves.

In Chapter 31 the sexual health promotion officer tells of her, and her colleagues', desire to 'educate and inform young people about the real world, with the real choices they have to make'. Chapters 26 and 30 deal with the difficult question of building up trust and confidentiality.

The importance of good working relationships with young people themselves is discussed in the youth worker's account (Chapter 27). Phil Creed sees his role as one of support rather than leadership, and discovered that allowing young people more of a say in the organisation and running of their club made it more 'secure' and 'relevant'.

On a more personal level, Marie's experiences of fostering young women also details the importance of establishing trusting working relationships (Chapter 25). In Marie's case, she wants 'to create not only an atmosphere where as four women we can respect and trust each other, but most importantly an atmosphere where everyone can feel safe'.

In any working environment, relationships with fellow workers and management can influence practice in either a positive or a negative way. In 'Accused' (Chapter 32) a residential social worker tells of his experience as a gay man being 'outed'. The encouraging support he received when dealing with external threats soon turned to disillusionment when he was subjected to verbal and physical abuse from the young people in his care.

His experience links with another area of work that needs to be acknowledged in respect of both working colleagues and young people: understanding discrimination. In Chapter 29 two black residential social workers talk of how 'there seemed to be absolutely no attention paid to the needs of young black people.' They highlight how such subconcious racism (that people 'seemed to think that it was racist even to consider that there was a difference') spilled over into their working relationships.

Conclusion

Young people should not be viewed as a homogeneous group. They experience society in very different ways. They hold a variety of views about what is 'right' and 'wrong'. Yet they do not necessarily see themselves as victims. Nor are their experiences always that different from adults'; they too have to confront poverty, lack of respect, social indifference and prejudice and ignorance.

They are pressed to conform, and some rebel. They are labelled, exploited, ignored and at times abused – both openly and covertly. In all this the care, nurturing and support of adults is of real importance. For some young people it might make the difference between 'success' and 'failure'.

As in any presentation of real-life experiences and opinions, there will undoubtedly be claims that you, and indeed we the editors, might not agree with. The issues covered in this book are the subject of intense debate and disagreement: this is inescapable. Yet we have enjoyed bringing the contributions in this volume together and we hope you find them as interesting and as stimulating as we have done.

Daren Garratt
Jeremy Roche
Stanley Tucker
The Open University

PART 1

BEING AND BELONGING

Identities

1
Culture Plus

Here Deb and Glazey talk about their experiences of being a young person in today's society.

Deb: Youth culture as political expression

I like too many different types of music to be able to *label* myself as anything. Other people don't seem to have too much trouble though. 'Crusty' is the main thing they tend to call me.

I started to form my own identity when I was still at school. I'd have been about 13 or 14. The teachers' immediate response was to keep on at me to dress smart, 'cos I'd have multicoloured plaits in my hair, I'd rip my tie an' stuff . . . Then I think their attitude towards me changed a bit. Like they kept telling me I'd never get a proper job. They just seemed to assume I'd 'gone off the rails' and they kicked me out eight weeks before our exams 'cos I'd had my eyebrow pierced.

There was about four of us in the whole school that were dressing similar and listening to the same things. The rest were into Take That. I liked the more political bands like The Levellers and Back to the Planet. But I've always liked the Sex Pistols and stuff like that . . . and Bob Marley 'cos my uncle was really into him.

You don't just sort of wake up one day and think, 'I know! I'll get piercings and dye my hair and look *weird.*' It's just something you want to do . . . y'know, you *identify* with the way other people who look like that *think*. The thing that appealed to me most was you see all these 'crusties' and travellers, and they seem so *free*. And everything they stood for, I agreed with. Y'know, I thought, 'Why am I dressing like a twat when I believe in all this stuff?'

Most of society's crap anyway. People are really narrow minded. I walk down the street and they're all staring and sniggering, and I think that's so sad. Have they got nothing better to do than talk about me? And it's always people who don't know me who make these judgements. If I went for a job now, it'll be like, 'Oh. Well we'll take you on if you don't wear eyeliner and take that *thing* [piercing ring] out of your lip.' And I'd be like, 'Fuck you. If you can't accept me as I am, then sod ya.' I wouldn't want to work for someone like that.

It's stupid, because like you go into a shop, and everyone's watching, thinking 'thieving little git'. It makes you sick. One of my mates went to that new Tesco's. He was walking round, and he had a pair of jeans on with them little pockets. They accused him of nicking a bottle of sherry! They kept having a go at him, and he was like, 'Look, you can search me. I ain't got anything.' All that 'cos of the way you look.

What I'm trying to get across with the way I look is the exact opposite to the way these people react to me. My ideals are totally against violence. We're more peaceful than most people, yet we get the blame when anything goes wrong. The press and the TV are always giving people like travellers a really bad name. Even stupid soaps like 'Home and Away'. If there's gonna be a 'bad guy' he's got to have long hair and a leather jacket and dreadlocks. Stuff like that just makes society worse, don't it? In 'Emmerdale Farm' there was that place full of people with dread-locks, and they were fighting. In real life, if you go to demos, they'll be the most peaceful people out of the whole lot.

A lot of the time I feel really vulnerable, just because of the way I look. Y'know, you've got people walking past you with kids, and the kids are totally fine with us, but the woman'll grab their hand and snatch 'em away as though we're gonna eat 'em or some-thing.

I think if I do affiliate myself with anything, then it is the travellers and 'crusties', 'cos there's so many families breaking up, that people are looking for *artificial* tribes now. When you're at places like festivals there's so many of ya, and everyone's alright. It *is* like a massive family. Except Glastonbury. That's gone really shit now. It's just full of football hooligans. And that really gets on my nerves. I don't like to say 'trendies', but I suppose that's what they are really – y'know, if they hate us and the way we look so much, why have they started taking over places like Glastonbury? One minute, they're like, 'Oooh! Weirdos', but as soon as they think it's fashionable, they all start dressing like this. Then as soon as they don't think it's fashionable any more, they'll be calling us weirdos again. They don't understand. They don't even listen to the lyrics of the songs. They don't seem to understand that people actually believe in what they're doing. It's a lot more than music. It's a lifestyle.

Glazey: Youth culture and the pursuit of pleasure

I started going to raves when I was about 20, in about 1992.

The first one I went to was illegal 'cos it was in a squatted flat in London, but I didn't think I was doing anything particularly political or subversive. It was just a change from going to the pub on a Saturday night.

It's definitely changed since then. You got more of a buzz off the scene being illegal, I think. Like the first time I was standing outside in the queue, and there was a riot van going past with loads of police in it. It was obviously an illegal party, but they'd probably got better things to do than break it up.

Nowadays there aren't as many 'free' parties about 'cos things get busted up more 'cos of the Criminal Justice Act. 'Paying' parties are more popular now. I don't think there's as much of a sub-cultural feeling about the dance movement as other groups. You get it a bit, but then again you get *so* many different types of people at an all-nighter, and they're all there for their own different reasons. There's no real defining label.

For me, part of going out is to do the drugs and smoke a bit of pot. The music and the drugs definitely go hand in hand. Then again, I listen to 'techno' at home and I don't have to get smashed, y'know. I *did* try to go clean after the New Year and give up doin' Es and speed. I didn't last one party! I lasted about two hours I think! The problem is, though, the media have pounced on the drug thing and blown it all out of proportion. I mean, look at the Leah Betts thing. It's bad that somebody died, but they seem to have just sensationalised that to sell their papers. I don't understand it. I remember when I went to that first party and I told the folks what I was going to. The first thing they said was, 'You didn't take any drugs did you?', and I said, 'No of course I didn't!' But that attitude's changed now, 'cos I go to them that often. Their attitude to *drugs* hasn't changed, but on a

Saturday tea-time all they say is, 'Are you going to be out all night tonight?', so I don't get any hassle or anything.

It's definitely more a hedonistic thing than say the discos I went to at the beginning of the nineties. The people at all-nighters all want to have a good time and dance and meet people. It's not like getting pissed and coming on to some woman. There's a real group feeling there. There's no bad vibes, it's all good vibes, and that's probably to do with Es and the feelings they generate. Y'know, you feel totally safe at these events. I've been going three or four years and I've never seen any hassle, I've never had any hassle. You get so used to not being alert to violence and trouble, that it doesn't even cross your mind. And the thing is, I think idiots and 'laddish' troublemakers *do* go, but they're outnumbered! *They're* probably the ones who feel out of place so they keep a low profile. It's not like your average nightclub.

The first thing I look for in a party is what the music's going to be like, and if I don't like it then I won't go. Now, that's not always been the case, because at the start I didn't know that much about the music. For me it *is* a musically orientated thing. Good music and going out with your mates.

The worst thing about it is going to work at 7.30 on a Monday morning. Especially if I've been smoking all day Sunday and not managed to get any sleep. That's a killer!

Interviews by Daren Garratt
The Open University

2

Kicking the Boundaries

Vicki, Jenny and 'Guisey' are women footballers. Here they talk about how football influences their lives.

Vicky's story

I'm 15 years old and I play in the under-17 squad for Wolverhampton Wanderers Women's Football Team. I've been interested in football all my life, y'know, playing with the lads an' that. When my sister saw an advert for the team in the paper I went to the trials. That was about two years ago.

I play football at school with the lads in PE, and I've never had any problems really. We have sports assessments, and they assess me like they would a boy. Y'see, from year 10 you can choose what you want to do in PE, and I thought, well, I want to play football. Then, come year 11 football was an option again so I did it. I was the only girl out of 22 lads. I still am. The lads are alright though. They treat me like they would normally. They talk to me about football, and I just feel like one of them. It's really good. Really good.

I mean, every week when I go back to school, my PE teacher asks about the Wolves and how we got on at the weekend. The teachers never come and see us, though. They live too far away. But they're interested in it, they ask me about it.

Jenny and 'Guisey' in conversation

Jenny (27) and 'Guisey' (28) also play for Wolverhampton Wanderers Women's Football Team. Here are their views on how the game and attitudes towards it have changed over the last 10 years.

> *Jenny*: When we first started playing about eight years ago, nobody thought we were good enough. The blokes used to come down when I was playing for Droitwich and they never took it seriously. Now that we're in the league, though,

people do actually come down and watch. It's getting better.
The standards have gone up.

Guisey: There was never a premier league or anything like that.
Just park football. Y'know, 11 girls turning up, booting the
hell out of each other and going home. But now we're on the
telly, in *The Times*. We've got a brilliant pitch, a brilliant set-
up, and a youth policy. The girls are playing just as much as
the boys now. We were brought up playing football anyway,
so it was nothing for us to come here and put a strip on.
When I was a kid I never knew there were women's teams. I
didn't start playing till I was 22, and that was really old. I'd
only ever played hockey. That was the only aggressive sport
that was available to me.

Jenny: I think women are coming into football more and more.
Obviously it's being televised a lot more; the England
women's team have just had good coverage on the telly. I
think it's going to be big in years to come.

Guisey: We're all in with the FA [Football Association] now, it's
not the WFA [Women's Football Association] any more. All
our fines and everything go through the same channels as the
men's, which is a big breakthrough. We're not seen as a
separate sport. We're all in this together.

Jenny: Which is good in a way, but if you get fined, or banned
or anything . . .

Guisey: . . . It's a lot more money!

Jenny: Yeah! And if a woman gets banned for five matches
that's half her season gone, but in the men's league that
might only be a week, so it's worse in that way.

Guisey: Some of the refs are patronising. Y'see, we now have
Class 1 refs, and they turn up and they just, well for a start,
they don't book enough players. They just seem to take the
mickey out of us. They don't take it seriously.

Jenny: Some'll do it. Some are quite strict, but with some you
can get away with too much.

Guisey: Like today, I knew I could get away with things and not
get a yellow card, and that's wrong. But that's the standard of
the referees. They think it's a joke. Instead of admiring
women's football and seeing it for what it is – and there's a
lot of skill involved – they just come here and think, 'Oh, it's
an easy £12/£20', or whatever. It's just extra money for
them. We should be classed the same as the men. Just
because we're women playing football shouldn't matter. We're
playing *football*, and football's got the same set of rules
whether you're a boy, a girl, a man or a woman. It's still the

same set of rules. It's not only the officials though. You get it at work as well. I work for the Post Office which is male dominated anyway, and some of the blokes just won't talk to you about football. They think women shouldn't know things about football; their place is behind the sink or the cooker, and they will not talk about football to you. Some men just don't want to know.

Jenny: You can't convince 'em. Where I work, though, the lads always ask how I've got on, 'cos they've begun to go around and watch women's football matches. Whereas you'll get people who don't even go to the matches and they'll say we're crap, basically because they haven't seen us play. I think everyone should just come down and have a look for themselves, 'cos I'm sure everyone's surprised by what they see.

Guisey: I used to work in a factory, and on a dinner-time we'd get a ball, go to one of the empty spaces and play football. I used to have guys come and try to take my legs 'cos I'd taken the ball around them. They had a real problem with women beating them to the ball and taking them on. They think women playing football is a joke, but it's not a joke. We want to do it. We ain't going to sit at home breeding and banging babies out. We don't want to do that, we want to be on a pitch playing football.

Jenny: If I stopped playing I wouldn't know what to do with myself.

Guisey: Football is my life. All my social life revolves around football, and that's a big commitment, y'know. At least three nights a week. So we have to go to work, do the housework *and* play football. Men don't have that problem. Yeah, they have to work, but they don't have to do their own housework, and they can still come out, play football and piss all their money against the wall. We can't do that. We've got responsibilities. We've got commitments. Some of the women have got kids. Some of the women have got husbands, *understanding* husbands who let them come out. But if I didn't have sport I'd be nothing. It's as simple as that.

Interviews by Daren Garratt
The Open University

3

Why Do You Think of Me Like That? Understanding Dyslexia

This chapter deals with the impact that dyslexia can have on an individual's life chances and educational opportunities. It also looks at how dyslexia is responded to by some within the education system.

Infancy

I didn't actually discover I was dyslexic until I was in my second year at Newcastle Polytechnic. Before then I didn't really know what it was. When I was 3, I had to see a speech therapist 'cos I didn't say any words. I just made noises and no one could understand me. All the kids used to chase me down the street impersonating me. Although I wouldn't speak, I was already really artistic, but because I couldn't express myself verbally I used to bite my hands. I was so frustrated, but I was still only a child.

When I started school I had a lot of problems 'cos the teachers thought I wasn't trying. This caused me to have aggressive tantrums and I'd always be fighting. I was about 7 when I stopped seeing the speech therapist, and up until then, school made allowances for me. As soon as I stopped having therapy, though, they'd say I never concentrated, that I wasn't good at anything, and that I'd *never* be good at anything. They never offered any help or encouragement, and dyslexia was never mentioned at all.

My mum thought the problem was that I couldn't read. I'd get all my letters mixed up and it was difficult having a conversation with me 'cos I'd stop in the middle of a sentence and stutter over words. The teachers never had patience with me, but I suppose that was because they had a lot of other kids to worry about. It got to the point where I never really spoke to anyone. I'd got no confidence.

Secondary school

At secondary school, because there were a lot more kids, there were obviously quite a few kids who were seen as being not very bright. We were all put into the same groups. I started to get into a lot of trouble at that time. I was really violent, but I honestly didn't care. One time I went to school drunk and my dad had to come from work, pick me up and take me home. In the end a school counsellor had to come and ask my mum what the problem was *at home*! They were certain that my behaviour could only be due to an unsettled family life. From that point I had to see a counsellor every week.

Then, on one occasion a teacher phoned home and advised me to take up an out-of-school activity, so from the age of 14 I started an art evening class. I went one night a week and it really helped me. I'd loved art since I was a child, but the teachers never encouraged the things that I *was* good at. Then, once I'd started the classes, another teacher phoned and told my mum that there was no need for me to do this extra art 'cos my work was good enough at school! I kept going though. My mum was trying really hard to help me solve my problems, and the teachers just turned around and said she was doing the wrong thing.

Once I started going to art classes I stopped getting into trouble. This was the last year at school, and I'd totally settled down. As a result they thought I was on drugs or sniffing glue (I found out later that this was basically because I never spoke to the teachers). The only teacher to ever help me was the English teacher. He told my mum I was too mature to be at school, and that was why the teachers never took me seriously. He said I had a load of good and interesting ideas, but I couldn't get them across on paper. But again, dyslexia was *never* mentioned, and being constantly told in school that you're no good and naughty is disastrous to your confidence.

Going to college

Art college was the best thing that happened to me. I started to develop a bit more confidence, 'cos no one knew anything about my background. They just judged me on the strength of my work. There wasn't much writing involved.

The first time I made something I was convinced I couldn't do it. Once I'd done it, though, the other students thought it was the best thing they'd seen, and the teacher said I shouldn't put myself down so much. But I still couldn't accept it when people would say, 'Oh, that's brilliant. You're really clever.'

The teachers at college could see I had a lot of talent, and it was the first time anyone within the education system understood my lack of confidence. It was the first time I'd encountered a lot of people recognising my talent, and recognising that if I was playing around I wouldn't learn anything. I ended up being spokesperson for my year, talking to the lecturers about the students' problems, etc. I still had a minor speech impediment but that disappeared after a while.

When I was 14 and being grounded a lot, hearing political bands like the Ex and Chumbawamba on the radio got me thinking. I could understand what people were saying to me. I just had problems communicating my ideas and thoughts back to them. College really understood that.

Higher education

Newcastle Polytechnic proved a bit of a problem. The emphasis was on the academic and to be seen to be good at art there, you had to be very good at *talking* about art. So, if like me you were crap at talking, they just thought you didn't know what you were doing. A lot of my work is very political and humorous, and though I knew why I was doing these things, the fact that I couldn't express my ideas verbally meant that my work wasn't valued by people.

It was in the second year when one of my lecturers recognised that I had trouble with my essays and she arranged for me to be tested for dyslexia. I picked up a leaflet and I couldn't believe what they were saying. Did I have problems leaving a crowded room? Did I feel anxious reading aloud or talking on the telephone? Did I have problems with money? This was me!

Discovering I was dyslexic really helped me. It boosted my confidence, in that I was able to excuse my actions, especially where money was concerned. People suddenly became more tolerant and helpful when I explained my situation.

The polytechnic lecturers still didn't seem to realise that dyslexia affects conversation, counting money and confidence. But apart from that, the polytechnic was very helpful. They cut my final dissertation from 10,000 to 3,000 words, gave me a separate exam room, and a longer time to complete my exam papers. They even offered me £3,000 to buy a computer. That's because dyslexia's viewed as a disability now. The education authority actually paid for my dyslexia lessons, which really helped me. They taught me the rules of language – the old way of teaching. I was shown cards with letters or drawings on them and I was taught how to put sounds to them. Y'know, the sort of thing I suppose most people have done since childhood, but was just beyond me. I can't comprehend words if I've never seen them before. I don't understand how someone can just do that naturally. I write as I talk, and as a result I've no comprehension of the structure of language. Then again, I never read. It doesn't seem natural to me.

Since I've left Newcastle I've been a lot happier 'cos I don't have to read or write anything. I just listen to music, draw, and I have an art studio where I make things. Being dyslexic isn't all negative. I've got an amazing memory which over-compensates for my other failings. I can remember trivial things from years ago in amazing detail. Not so long ago I went back to tell one of my school teachers that I'd finally discovered I was dyslexic, and how relieving it was to have some understanding of why school had been so truly horrible. All they could say was, 'Oh, forget about it. It probably wasn't as bad as you imagined.'

It's only been in the last six months that I've started to admit that I'm good at drawing. It's taken me 23 years to realise that I can do something, basically because there was someone putting me down all the time. It's hard to think I could ever get over the experience I had at school, but I have and I think I'm a much better person for it. I still have problems speaking in social groups, but I've got a lot more confidence and I'm very positive in my outlook and the way I live my life.

Claire
Interview by Daren Garratt
The Open University

4

Space, Respect and Support

Amir is 16 years old. Since 1993 he has been in a wheelchair. In this account he talks about his experiences as a disabled person in the education system.

Primary school life

The teachers in my primary school were very kind and considerate. They did a lot to help me and gave me support and built up my confidence. The main problem though was with the school building itself. At the time I could walk on sticks, but it was difficult to get about in the school. There were no ramps and things like that. It was a big school and sometimes I had to walk right across it. I found that hard. I can particularly remember all the steps. It was an old school with new parts built on to it. There were steps everywhere. Walking about like that caused me great difficulties, because I became very tired indeed.

Thinking about secondary school

When it came to choosing a secondary school, I thought carefully about what kinds of things I would want there to support me. Lifts and ramps were vital, and help if you needed it from members of staff. I met with someone from the education department to discuss what school I wanted to go to. I didn't think a special school would be helpful: it's important to go to a 'normal' school if possible. Someone like me should have no trouble fitting in, provided they can get help when it's needed. I wanted the chance to be with everyone else that I knew.

School design

I think my school – Cradley High School – is really good for people in wheelchairs. Anybody designing a school should look at it, because there is a lot they could learn. The design of the school makes it easy for someone in a wheelchair to get around. There are wide corridors downstairs and a lift to take you to the top floor. There are also plenty of ramps to make life that much better. I am also able to use a disabled toilet, which again is really important for anyone in a wheelchair because it can save embarrassment and problems.

The classroom design is also really good. The tables I sit at are just the right height for me. Although I do have problems in science lessons doing experiments because of the difficulty of using the equipment on the main benches. This is something that could be improved. I think equipment needs to be bought with disabled young people in mind. Even if there is not a disabled person in the school at the time, if you see that the equipment meets your needs you are more likely to choose that school. Also, anyone designing a school needs to remember they are really busy places, particularly when you are changing lessons. Some of the corridors upstairs are a bit too narrow. I can see that worrying someone in a wheelchair. I sometimes just have to wait until the crush has finished. It's not a big problem for me, but it could be for someone else.

Support

As a disabled person the important thing I want to say is that I want support when I need it – but I don't need it all the time. Sometimes you can get enough help from your mates. And while they are helping you, we talk as well. Adult help isn't always needed. It's important to remember that.

I think the teachers in my school are really good. They seem to understand my needs. They talk to me and I can always go and ask most of them for extra help if I need it. The important thing for me is that they don't let me get away with things just because I am disabled. They expect me to do the work, and if I don't, I expect to be told off. That's the way it should be. I have confidence in them because of this. I also have a welfare assistant who is there if I need to move around the school or want help. Most of the time that's fine, but I also like having the opportunity to do things for myself now that I'm older. So there is another thing to bear in mind: as I grow older I do want to try more things. That's the same for everyone I should think.

Getting to and from school is not really a problem for me. The council are good; they provide a taxi every day and the driver is brilliant! At home, of course, my mum and dad and sister really support me. My uncles are great too, always sending presents that would be useful to someone in a wheelchair. A while ago my uncle sent me a cordless intercom system that I can move around the house. My house is also really good now. I used to have my bed downstairs in the lounge. I wasn't too keen on that. I wanted a space of my own. I also used to bash the house about a bit with my wheelchair. You should see the holes I have made in the doors! But the council have built a small extension on to the house, and I now have my own bedroom, shower and toilet and study area. All this is really important for my schoolwork. You need your own space to study in. A place that is away from the rest of the family when you want it. I think all disabled people should have this kind of facility if they want it.

Work experience

My work experience was really good but before I went for it, I had to make a choice. I think in some ways people wanted me to stay in school and work there. I didn't want that. I wanted to try something that was outside the school. I went to the Argos Superstore and the staff there were absolutely great. They supported me, but gave me real jobs to do. I had my own work to get on with. Some of it was in the office, and some of it was on the shop floor. Once when I first went there, this member of staff who did not know me came up to me in the shop and said, 'Can I help?' He didn't realise I was working there. I suppose that says something about who you expect to be working in a shop. I just laughed, it was funny.

In Argos, the shop and the offices are designed to be used by disabled people. You can fit in right from the start. Special things don't have to be done for you. Shops like Argos I think are looking at what disabled people need now. The design of the whole place makes moving about, choosing things and working a lot easier. I think this is part of the fact that there is more effort being made to treat disabled people better and make buildings better for them. There is still a long way to go. Things like buses, if it's not 'ring and ride', are difficult. But you have to start somewhere. Other things are important to encourage disabled people to apply for jobs. Saying things like an office has been adapted, or putting in an advert that applications from disabled people are welcome, is very important.

Further education

I'm just starting to make my mind up about further education. At the moment I hope to do my A levels and then go on to university. I think in the end I would like to be in the Diplomatic Service, I have had a look at what you require for that.

The layout of my future college is really important to me, and so are the subjects available. I talked to staff at one college that did not have a lift. They said I would have had to do all my work on the ground floor. I was willing to give one of my subjects up, but it still didn't work out. I could have got a place there with my estimated grades, but they just weren't willing to do much for me. Did it make me angry? No, not really, it just made me feel sad for them. Someone at that place needs to decide on how they are going to respond to people in wheelchairs or anyone who has trouble moving around easily. You can't change everything you want to do just to fit the layout of a building.

The place where I am likely to go now is completely different. First, they have had disabled people there before and so they are used to meeting their needs. When I spoke to someone on the telephone they were enthusiastic, like they really wanted me to go there. When disabled people have been to a place before it makes you that much more confident. Another thing is how they will be able to organise my lessons. Everything will be in one building block, and it has lifts and ramps. That means I don't have to travel miles around the campus. I think they respect the disabled person's right to independence. All universities and colleges across the country should try and encourage disabled people like this.

A message about treatment

I want to finish by saying something about how disabled people want to be treated. They want respect and fairness. They will give it back when it is given to them. Disabled people are capable of doing things for themselves. They just need time and space like anyone else. If they don't ask for help it is probably because they don't want it at that time. When disabled people want help they will ask, they are more than capable of doing that.

Amir

5

Young Parents

Jez and Gen explore their experiences of and ideas about being young people. They also talk about how society in general reacts to them.

Jez's story

I am 21, dependent on the welfare system and three months pregnant. It was a real shock when we found out – I thought I'd got a kidney infection – but it only took a few hours before we started feeling positive about having a child. I have been with my boyfriend five years and living with him for three, so we know what a committed relationship we have. I couldn't have a child in an unstable relationship. It just wouldn't be fair on anyone.

Our friends and families are really pleased for us. They know how happy we are, so everyone's really positive, but people who don't even know us seem to have very definite opinions about the situation. For example, I get called 'Mrs' at the antenatal clinic. I did find it funny until I realised it meant they still didn't really approve of unmarried mothers. We find it odd because we're not married, not because we're not committed, but because we don't believe in the concept of marriage. Most of our friends don't either, so it looks like there'll be thousands of unmarried mothers about the place eventually. I suppose the medical profession will just have to come to terms with it.

Another major problem I've come across is people's opinions on whether or not I'll be a fit mother, simply because we haven't got much money. Once again, these tend to be people who don't know us very well, but *that* doesn't seem to bother them. They think there should be a minimum level of income before you're allowed children. As if only the rich will become good parents. We *know* how much we love our baby already, and we know that money doesn't really come into the equation, so we just ignore the comments. But it does hurt that people can be so shallow.

I always thought pregnancy would be a wonderful experience, and inside I feel great, but all these outside influences keep spoiling things. At the antenatal classes they keep talking about the *violence* of the birth, and the *tearing*, the *stitches*, the *pain*. I sit there thinking, 'Hang on, it can't be all that bad. What about the end result?' Already they want to scare me with horror stories, and I've still got six months to go.

I'm treating the birth and my child as the light at the end of the tunnel. Things *are* going to be hard, but I know it will all be worth it when we can meet our baby.

Gen's story

I first became pregnant in 1988, so I'd have been about 19. Rich and I were already married by this time and living in a high-rise block. Before we moved there we'd been staying at my nan's, which was OK. We just never had any privacy or space for the two of us. So it was alright in our flat in the beginning, but as soon as we knew I was pregnant we applied to the council to be rehoused. It took 'em 16 months to actually find us somewhere – Sean was seven months old!

At first they said they weren't going to move us at all, because there was a waiting list, but we'd already been on the list ages. I don't know if you know, but what the council do is give you 'three chances'. They offer you three choices of property, and if you don't accept them you get shoved to the bottom of their waiting list again. They offered us these really crappy places; the first one was really horrible so we turned that down. Then we were offered another and that was *worse*! Finally we were offered one that was just like the others with really loud neighbours and horrible bratty kids. We couldn't bring Sean up in places like that. It wouldn't have been fair.

So after being told that we wouldn't get out of our flat for years, then being offered really bad choices, we were told we'd have no chance of moving again. That was when somebody suggested we write to our local councillor. Basically we just gave him all our details, told him our situation and that we didn't think it was fair to be made to raise a child in the environment we were in. We even sent the thing to the wrong person, but the right bloke must've got hold of it somehow, 'cos within four weeks we got moved to this beautiful three-bedroomed semi.

Benefits
We had a lot of trouble with social security, and we're *still* having problems with housing benefit now, and I'm just about to

have my third baby. But the dole was terrible. When we first met, Rich was working, but he got laid off. They put him on all these different schemes to try and get him back to work, but they were no good. They just gave him an extra tenner on top of his income support. And it was just so much hassle. We were always having giros going missing, and they were really reluctant to help us out or issue replacements or anything. It was like they didn't want to give us any money at all if they could help it. We even applied for loans 'cos we needed a cooker and a bed, but they were asking something silly in return payment. It was unaffordable. There was no way we could have done it. It was just ridiculous. Same with housing benefit. There was continual mix-ups over what we should be paid, and as I said, we're still having the same problems with them now, for one reason or another.

Support

We got no support from social services whatsoever. No advice or anything. Supposedly, the government had various extra payments we were entitled to, but we never got none of that really. They don't tell you about these things.

It was the same with us being married. I don't know why, but if you claim you're living together but unmarried you get more money. They seem to presume that once you're married you don't need help any more. And that's just not true. You're not seen to have any privileges. We found that out when we were on the council's waiting list: everyone's just lumped in together. I think you do have a slight advantage if you're married and you rent privately, but a lot of people don't know you can do that and still get housing benefit. They don't realise that it's possible to get into a really nice terraced house for a lot less money. There's some parents at Sean's school who've got five kids and are stuck in a tower block. And it's mainly because no one tells them what's available.

As far as the authorities were concerned we were out on a limb. All our support came from our parents. I think they were a bit nervous at first, just because we were so young. Mum said I must be mad, but they were OK really. They bought us loads of things, and were there if we needed them, but they never poked their noses in what really was *our* affair. I know I've dwelled a bit on the non-existent support offered by the DSS, but we didn't have a *bad* time. I wasn't worried or scared about becoming a parent. I think I was more bemused than anything! Money was something of a worry, but then it always is.

No, being pregnant isn't a problem, it's once they're born you've got to worry. Only joking.

Interviews by Daren Garratt
The Open University

6

Racism and Respect: Black Pride, Black Youth and Black Workers

This chapter is concerned to explore the issue of black pride and the particular issues that face workers in its promotion with young people.

I'm a black woman, and I used to be a teacher in a secondary school where most of the students are black, and most of the staff are white. On one occasion when I trudged into the staffroom about to make my weary way home, I saw a young black woman, an ex-pupil of the school, who had come to visit one of her former teachers. Out of the blue, she stopped her conversation and asked me whether I was actually a teacher. When I said I was, she gazed at me for a moment or two, and a slow smile spread across her face. Finally she said, almost to herself: 'Respect guy. Respect.' Smiling broadly, I walked out of the staffroom. By the time I got downstairs though, I was crying. At the time I had no idea why.

In thinking about writing on black pride, this incident has come back repeatedly into my mind, bringing with it all sorts of questions. What opportunities do young people have to make connections between blackness and self-respect when they live in a racist society? Moreover, what are some of the particular issues facing black workers in white-dominated institutions when we work to provide those opportunities?

BUILD and TRY

I discussed these and other questions with three black youth workers in Nottingham, all of whom work in specialist services for black young people. Kevin and Joy work at Team Resources for Youth (TRY), an organisation which was set up in 1981 by Nottinghamshire County Council to identify and meet the needs of black young people where other mainstream conventional youth clubs had failed. Panya works for BUILD Nottingham Mentor Programme, which was set up in 1991 and has the primary purpose of pairing black young people with an older black professional who can encourage and support the young person in achieving their academic goals and entering their chosen career.

Naming racism

Racism is the persistent backdrop to both of these projects. Both are responding to the fact that, for example, African-Caribbean children are being suspended from Nottinghamshire schools at five times the rate of their white counterparts; the number of reported deaths of black young people in police custody is not only high but is increasing; and levels of unemployment and underemployment amongst young African-Caribbean men in particular are twice those of their white counterparts.

These are not simply cold statistics. They are hard realities faced by black young people and workers day by day. The pain of knowing that five black students at once were suspended just before their final exams was, I know, one of the factors that finished off my teaching career. In the past fortnight I have had to watch two friends living in two different parts of the country grieving over the emotional and educational injury which their children were experiencing through the negligence or directly racist actions of teachers and other young people: 'the system is mashing up my child' one of them said. And on top of this, the huge cuts in resources (including the withdrawal of Section 11 funding), which have effectively put an end to a range of much-needed services for black people, are a constant burden to workers in specialist projects like TRY and BUILD.

Now as black people we must keep talking about these everyday experiences and we must keep quoting these well-known statistics. This is not only because there is a need at times to release that buildup of anger and hurt (although this reason would of itself be sufficient). In my conversation with Joy and Kevin it became clear that the aspect of their work which has changed the most is the low priority now being given to anti-racist work and the provision of information on black history. I accept that anti-racism training as it was conceived in the 1980s often (though not always) did adopt a simplistic approach to racism and to black history (see, for example, Gilroy, 1992; 1993: 187–201). Moreover, many black practitioners know from painful experience that too much anti-racism training has relied on black workers leading one-off workshops in which they found themselves standing in the line of fire when white workers expressed not only their racism, but also their anger and frustration over larger changes in institutional policy. Ultimately:

White workers should be addressing racism for white workers. (Kevin)

Nevertheless, a clear and insistent naming of the racism in our lives is still a necessary strategy for combating that racism and is therefore a prerequisite for building self-respect. The recognition now rightly being given to other oppressions (gender, disability etc.) in fact makes it imperative to analyse racism even more closely as it interacts with sexism, heterosexism etc. and becomes ever more subtle.

Role modelling and mentoring

Black workers need to be able to pass on to black young people both our experiences of racism and our strategies for struggling against it. In this way when others tell you you're a nigger, 'your elders tell you you're black, and they can tell you how to deal with it' (Panya). This aspect of mentoring or role modelling is central to the work that BUILD does.

Mentoring relies on an identification by the young person that:

> this person comes from the same place as me, gone through the same school system, encountered the same problems . . . they're just members of the ordinary community . . . if this person can achieve this there's no reason why I can't. (Panya)

And yet this need for identification with other black people, without a firm definition of what blackness is, can have the effect of putting up barriers around blackness using criteria which are often contradictory and therefore impossible to really satisfy.

> Is it about the levels of melanin in our skin? Is it about whether we're born in Africa, St Kitts, Barbados, Jamaica? Is it about whether we dress in a particular style and fashion? Is it about whether we eat a particular style of food? Is it about how we speak? What is black? . . . There's all these debates about levels of blackness, and you're not black enough, or I'm not black enough . . . If you were black you wouldn't have said that, and if you were black you wouldn't behave like that. (Kevin)

Two points come out of this for building black pride in young people. The first is about how the worker defines the young person as black. There is a high level of debate going on amongst black people about what blackness is. We are defining it and redefining it all the time in the way we live our lives, as well as the things we say, and the books we read, and the discussions we have, and above all the chances that we take. Young black people need to be given access to that debate and to be allowed to make their contribution:

What we do through our work is expose them to a range of things, and then give them the choices, because we can't make those decisions for them . . . All we try and do is encourage debate. (Joy)

I've attended several forums now, organised by both BUILD and TRY, in which black people, young and old, fell out with each other, rebuked each other, listened to each other, and learned from each other. Participation in the debate is, I feel, where black pride is actually built: the fact of our participation, whatever form it takes, shows us that we belong.

The second point is about how the young black person can define the worker's blackness. Role modelling requires the role model to stay 'real', that is to steer a course between 'supermodel' and 'no-model'. Panya, Kevin, and Joy were agreed that it was good for young people to see them as black professionals in their schools and in their communities, so that the young people know that 'there's somebody doing something' (Joy) and so that the young people can see that their teachers and other authority figures also know that there is somebody available to offer institutional backing if that authority is abused.

The black worker often forms a bridge between white-dominated institutions and black young people. This is a position of strength, but also of vulnerability. For at times the young person can reject the black worker because they work too closely with institutions that they do not trust (they are 'too white'). At other times the institutions can reject the black worker because they are too closely aligned with the rest of the black community and no longer represent an acceptable form of blackness (they are 'too black'). The complexity of this positioning requires complex strategies to deal with it, strategies which are worked out in practice each day, and which black workers need to share with each other. There are no overall or easy formulae for a chapter of this size to go into. The writing of people like bell hooks (1991 and 1994, for example) is worth reading as a start, but I feel that there is no substitute for linking in with other black workers from lots of different professional fields, and just talking.

Negating the negation

If you were out in the street and someone attacked one of you . . . would you then say no, she's not my sister, and be gone? (Joy)

The existence of racism, and the materiality of the suffering caused by it, remain a touchstone for work on the promotion of black pride. This is emphatically *not* a negative reactive thing. It is a process of:

> absorbing all negation in order to negate it . . . [because] a hasty affirmation, a premature sense of being accepted and affirmed as a full subject by the hegemony . . . is always in danger of being appropriated once again by the processes of hegemonic formation. (Jan Mohamed, 1990: 122–3)

Put more clearly, black pride for young people, and for black workers and elders, is this:

> Always question what you're told. Don't just take it on face value . . . Do not give up, keep on trying. Every bad experience you come across, make it work for the better. Channel it round, change it, and make it work for the better . . . If they say 'you can't do that' . . . you take that, you take it within you, and you turn it round, so that you can throw it back in their face. (Panya)

References

Gilroy, P. (1992) 'The end of antiracism', in J. Donald and A. Rattansi (eds) *'Race', Culture and Difference*, London: Sage.

Gilroy, P. (1993) *The Black Atlantic: Modernity and Double Consciousness*, London: Verso.

hooks, b. (1991) *Yearning: Race, Gender, and Cultural Politics*, London: Turnaround.

hooks, b. (1994) *Sisters of the Yam: Black Women and Self-Recovery*, London: Turnaround.

Jan Mohamed, A. (1990) 'Negating the negation as a form of affirmation in minority discourse: the construction of Richard Wright as subject', in A. Jan Mohamed and D. Lloyd (eds), *The Nature and Context of Minority Discourse*, Oxford: Oxford University Press.

Pat Patten
Freelance Writer

7

Incest Survivor

A personal account is given here of the experience of incest and one young woman's response to it as a 'survivor'. The idea is explored that it is possible to fight back and offer support to others who find themselves in similar circumstances.

When I was asked to write this report I didn't know where to start, it's hard to put your life into 'approximately 2,000 words!' I'm nearly 18 and was sexually and physically abused by my father and his friends. It was mainly a group thing, but happened individually between the two of us as well.

The things that happened to me are too horrific to describe in detail. Chances are people won't want to read it. A few years ago I phoned the NSPCC crying out for help, but they told me to 'stop lying and put the phone down'. There's more to my story than the stereotype of 'my dad comes into my room at night and touches me' and for that reason people tend to turn away. I only hope writing this will help other young people and prevent them from being dragged into the things I've experienced at home and on the street.

The hardest thing there has been for me to cope with as a result of being abused is the self-hatred I feel for myself. Self-hate is too big to put into words. It's always there, eating away at my insides. I can never punish myself enough – I want to hurt myself and get some of this pain out of me, and the only way I know how is to hurt myself. I can never get rid of the guilt, self-hate, and anger at myself that I feel and in the past the only way I've been able to control it is through anorexia/bulimia and self-harm. There have been times when people have told me I wouldn't see past my next birthday, but as I refused medical help, counselling or therapy there was nothing they could do. Ultimately the decision to recover had to be my own.

I don't hold any explanations as to why people allow food to control their lives, but what I do know is that it isn't as simple as the media portrays. I did not starve myself to be thin or look like

Kate Moss. Why I did is hard to explain. When I was 11 all I wanted to do was kill myself. I was tearing up my arms – I wanted to get some of this pain out of me, and the only way I knew was to hurt myself.

At the time I was taller than my friends and looked older (though I'm short and look young for my age now). Men were interested in me – not boys, but dirty old men who obviously recognised me as the weak, defenceless victim I felt I was. Having been abused by several adult members of my family I knew nothing but abuse and didn't even recognise it as that. What I did know was that I wanted it to stop and the only way I could imagine it would was by refusing to grow into this 'woman' my father was so excited about me becoming. I saw that being female made you accessible to abuse, I couldn't care less about being thin – I just didn't want to grow into what these bastards wanted me to. If I stopped eating, my periods stopped, I didn't grow and felt less like a woman.

Bingeing and vomiting was different. I always associated choking with oral sex. Bingeing made me feel like I was choking: it sounds strange but it made sense to me then to vomit after eating all this food.

I desperately wanted to escape my body. I always imagined there to be my body and me. My body acted, my mind disappeared and so I wanted, needed, to punish my body for allowing myself to be abused. Self-hate got to a point where all I ever wanted to do was hurt myself. I could never punish myself enough. For me there was a difference between self-hate and body hatred. I hated this body which I felt held me prisoner and longed to escape it. The only way I could escape was to starve myself, believing (subconsciously) if I starved and destroyed my body enough I'd finally be free. I hated the person inside even more. I felt like the only way to feel better was to punish myself – mainly by cutting up my arms. I wanted to break down and cry but I couldn't let go. I wanted to get angry, but I was scared if I did I'd simply explode. I felt so dirty and could never scrub the dirt away. I could never learn to like myself. It didn't matter how much or how hard I scrubbed the self-hate, dirt, guilt, they were all there eating away at my insides.

I felt like I was always going to be a victim of other people's power and control. I constantly used to ask myself, what is it that I am doing wrong, which makes people see how vulnerable I am? What did they see in me that indicates they can hurt and abuse me? I was convinced it was my fault – that each time I was raped or abused I must have done something to provoke the attack.

Maybe it would have been easier if my father were alive. One of the things that hurts the most is that I'll never get a chance to confront him with what he has done to me. Perhaps I would never have done, but to be able to get angry, to be a moody temperamental teenager would be better than this. I feel as though I have to confront so many taboos. To say I've been abused is hard enough, but when the abuser is now dead, suddenly anyone you try and tell thinks you're making a fuss. People aren't allowed to speak badly of the dead. When someone dies they are suddenly forgiven for all the bad things they have done; but I can't forgive him for raping and torturing innocent children, even if he is my father.

My father was registered disabled, although as a child I was naive enough to think you had to be in a wheelchair to be disabled and didn't recognise the nature or severity of his disabilities. To be honest I still don't. There's nobody I can ask – and so in many ways I still internalise this image of my father being the 'hero' my family see him as. All anyone can do is sing his praises. I guess this is my way of screaming at the world and telling them it's not like that.

When I was younger I used to frequently run away. I was running away from myself as much as the problems at home. I often slept rough in surrounding towns, rural places where homelessness wasn't recognised as a problem. There were no night shelters, day centres, soup kitchens; I felt so alone and there was no one to turn to and ask for help. I was scared if I told anyone where I was sleeping I'd be taken into care, so instead I used to just wander the streets rather than face the violence at home. I desperately wanted someone to love me, and the thing that made sleeping rough difficult was that not only did society reject me (for being homeless) but the people I met on the street were cold, unfriendly and suspicious of me. After a day they'd taken all my money, after a week I felt as though they'd taken all my self-worth.

I watched people get into drugs and prostitution and believe me when you are cold, hungry, miserable and alone you'd try anything. When some guy offered to pay me to have sex with him I reached breaking point. I left home so my body could become my own and nobody would abuse and violate it to their advantage. I said no, he beat me, I still refused, he held out a knife. Somehow I survived.

After that it no longer mattered to me – I felt like my body was never going to be my own and I'd never had any control. If a stranger asked me to go back with him I would. I wasn't naive, I knew what the score was and what he'd expect in return, but even though I was in my early teens (about 12 or 13), I really didn't care. I was so used to being raped and abused. It wasn't just for money. I needed to be loved, these men had chosen me. It sounds sick but it made me feel special. I had a bed for the night and had learnt to effectively shut out my feelings so the sex didn't hurt and I could do the sometimes sick things they asked me to do.

It was dangerous because prostitution was hidden and these weren't your typical punters. They were weirdos who noticed a young girl wandering alone at night. My age is what attracted them, the vulnerability which was so easy to take advantage of.

When I was 16 I went to Brighton with nothing but a sleeping bag and a change of clothes. My friend had just committed suicide and I was in an irrational state; I had to escape from everything and couldn't cope with life. I was half asleep in a doorway shivering with cold and flu and a group of travellers took me back to their squat. They all took off their coats to warm me up and wrapped me up in sleeping bags – without them anything could have happened to me. I was so cold, ill, upset I really didn't care.

The same year I went to London. It was the first place I've ever felt I belonged and I miss it so much because of that. For the first time in my life I was part of a society who accepted me for myself – people who'd look out for me if anything went wrong. The street brings people together and you look out for each other. Nobody else will.

I spent that year on and off the streets and last summer started selling *The Big Issue*. *The Big Issue* and Brighton taught me there was more to the streets than begging, drugs and prostitution, that was all I'd seen outside London. In London it's worse for drugs and prostitution – but because they aren't hidden problems it's easier to get help.

When you sell *The Big Issue* (or beg) you are telling people something about yourself, showing them you are in a vulnerable situation – homeless and asking them to help you help yourself. It's like being abused all over again when people ignore you, turn away, make insulting comments, or worse still physically or sexually assault you.

The worst thing I've found about the street is the number of people who die, I've seen so many of my friends abuse themselves (with drink, drugs, self-harm, suicide) to compensate for the abuse others have inflicted on them; it's a way of numbing the pain and stopping it from hurting any more. Unfortunately it's also danger-ous and life-threatening. Death has been such a huge issue for me to face. Every time someone dies it hurts so much, but because of the situations I'm in I have to get used to it. My friend Danny died of an AIDS related illness. It all terrifies me sometimes.

Nobody has ever been willing to listen to me – teachers at school, social services, the NSPCC – so I decided if nobody else would believe or help me I'd find a way to speak out against the abuse that dominated my childhood and which (I believe) forced me onto the streets. I started a newsletter which I hoped would give survivors a voice and would be somewhere to share ideas, experiences, writing, poetry, artwork etc. and a contact network to put survivors in touch with one another. Over 65 people (nation-wide) responded over the year and for a while it was working really well. The problem is though that it's a mainly 'underground' newsletter called *Breaking Free*. We have no money, no resources and because of this and the growing number of interested people, it's impossible to send it out to everyone without money for photocopying and postage. It's too much responsibility for me to handle on my own.

When *Breaking Free* started I never imagined there would be much response. I desperately wanted a voice and for somebody to hear it. I wanted to tell people what had happened to me as a child and what I knew was happening to hundreds of other children. Nobody wanted to listen and as I was pushed further into silence I felt more isolated and alone. There needed to be a voice for survivors and nobody was offering one. I hoped maybe the newsletter would. *The Big Issue* helped with photocopying and use of a computer, and You 2 with an address. I was naive and didn't think the newsletter would involve much responsibility, but it did. I was reading letters from people who like myself were hurting. I hadn't dealt with my own pain, I didn't know how to deal with anyone else's. I'd lie awake at night and worry if someone was alright. Having had close friends commit suicide I couldn't handle people writing to me and saying they wanted to die. I also got letters saying the newsletter was good and helping people, so I carried on thinking I could make it work.

At the moment I'm undecided whether to carry the newsletter on. Practically (resource-wise) it's impossible. Emotionally I just want to leave all this abuse shit behind me and get on with my life. I'm determined not to be a victim any more. Abuse doesn't have to be all negative and it's taught me some important things – like my body is my own and no one has a right to touch it unless I want them to. I'm streetwise enough to look after myself and have seen enough shit to appreciate things – silly things that people take for granted and don't notice, like sunny days.

Maybe I'm idealistic, but if enough people speak out then maybe society will eventually accommodate our needs.

Beverley

8

Beating Eating Disorders

Ann Cox used anorexia nervosa and bulimia nervosa as an emotional 'coping mechanism' for almost 28 horrific years, and has charted this period in her frank and powerful autobiography Autumn Dawn: Triumph over Eating Disorders *(1995). Here she talks a little more about how professionals working with young people may be able to detect, prevent and help beat the manifestation of this terrible* dis-ease.

An emotional hunger

I think the best way I'd put it is I became obsessive about the addictions I'd developed. I only became addicted in a desire to maintain the *buzz*. The reason for doing the damage, I didn't know. My head got filled with the addictions rather than the real issues in life, so I was kind of *denying reality* by trying to solve things.

It's so easy to get caught up in the symptoms when you're ill because you've taken, albeit subconsciously, the focus off the real issues in life. So I wasn't anxious about my parents, I wasn't worried about my friends. I was able to solve all those concerns with a 24-hour obsession with food, weight, shape and size. You get so caught up in how you're going to avoid the next meal, how you're going to get rid of it, how you're going to lose the weight, that your mind becomes so full of food and exercising that it's all too easy to see that as the actual problem as opposed to an emotional one.

I used to say, 'I want to be thin because I don't have to feel.' So not eating meant not feeling. Not eating meant numbing my emotions, but I got locked into not eating only meaning getting thin. I had tunnel vision; the symptom was the problem. I did not realise that the symptom was really the avenue for numbing myself.

As alcoholics do not necessarily drink because they like it, bulimics don't binge eat because they like it – it's a means to an end. In order to become a good anorexic, a good bulimic, a good alcoholic, you have to work at it, to make it work for you. Yes, it works in a destructive way, but it does work and it's vicious. You have to constantly work at it to get your rewards. Initially, just starving and losing weight gave me a buzz, but when my body got used to that, I had to combine starving and weight loss with addictive exercise. Then I had to increase the symptoms even more, so I took laxatives and diuretics, vomited and purged. A bit like the alcoholic who goes from one can (of beer) to 10 cans because one stops being enough. You get a kind of 'used to it' level, and that's exactly the same as an eating disorder. The difficulty is, an eating disorder is not recognised because of the behaviour level. The alcoholic who is drunk will be seen to be out of order, whereas an anorexic will not. But here am I talking about something that is perceived. But what about what goes on behind closed doors? Certainly with anorexia nervosa where the weight loss is horrific, or substantial, there is a very clear message. Unfortunately, the public tends to read the message as 'diet', but the message is very different; something is wrong.

Why?

No one develops anorexia nervosa or bulimia nervosa just 'like that'. You can't pinpoint the start. I earned the label 'anorexic' when my weight dropped substantially enough for me to be described as emaciated, or thin.

I was an only child and from the age of about 9 or 10 I went through what probably loads of adolescents fear anyway but which, for me, kind of just emphasised what I already felt: a great lack of confidence, a great lack of self-esteem. There was an emptiness there. I couldn't replace it with anything so I tried to fill that emotional void with food and what I'm sure the doctor would describe as 'comfort eating'. But it wasn't comfortable! I ate until I had a dreadful tummy ache, and going to bed with this tummy ache was easier than going to bed with this feeling of helplessness, hopelessness. It was an inside loneliness, 'cos if I shared it with my mother and father it was dismissed as a growing-up 'thing'. It wasn't allowed. So the seeds of my *self-dis-ease* were apparent very early on. As a result, I think eating disorders emanate, without doubt, from low self-esteem and low self-confidence.

I desperately wanted to be like everybody else, to be liked etc., and I had a feeling of differentness. When all my friends started going on diets I decided to join them solely to be one of the crowd. However I wasn't interested in slimming. I didn't need to lose weight. So I pretended to. It was a real sham – I just ate the diet toffees and then ate the meal as well! But being seen buying the toffees with them was like being one of them.

It's odd, with hindsight, that I should have joined them on that one thing (food) and later on in my life gone full tilt into eating disorders. But I see that as purely coincidental. It carries no great significance. After all, body image and food is a social thing. I think I chose the avenue of food, and this was because I was a war baby: I picked up my parents' attitude to food as something that should be respected and valued, so if I was going to punish myself then why not do it by taking away the one thing I loved? You see, I loved my food very much (and still do!) as does everyone with an eating disorder.

Obstinate resistance and denying the denial

The reason I had an obstinate resistance to all the signs that something was wrong was because I had a friend. It worked. This obsession with food filled up my head for 24 hours so I didn't have to think about my helplessness, my hopelessness, and other problems. I'd got a buzz! I was hooked, and it was great. And this is the great difficulty, especially with teenagers in the early years of anorexia. Until you get to the point where you're so desperately ill, it's very difficult to see anything problematic about something that creates such a buzz. How the hell have you got an enemy when you've got a friend like that? This is the obstinate resistance that an outsider is always faced with.

I think we're still in a world where any pamphlets on eating disorders present you solely with the symptoms. What to look for. And it's too late. You'll see the symptoms; it's before those symptoms manifest themselves that is the time. In the kind of work that I've done I've asked people and their parents and partners to say a little bit about how they were as children. And every time I hear them say, 'She always needed a bit of reassurance. She was always a bit unsure of herself and seemed to need encouragement rather a lot. In fact she would put herself down rather a lot saying "Everyone's much better than me."' I think it's that sort of language which is the thing that you've got to pick up on. If you've got a child in class saying 'everyone's better than me', now obviously that doesn't mean she's got an eating disorder or an addiction, but it means she's feeling a sense of inadequacy and you've got to spend time to listen to how she feels. If that inadequacy is dismissed then the reaction might be, 'Oh, I'm not allowed to feel like that' or 'I shouldn't feel like that' – in comes the guilt because you *do* feel like it. Just because you *shouldn't* feel like it doesn't mean you stop feeling like it. And because expressing it hasn't worked – it's been dismissed – you're gonna find a way to either repress it, depress it, or get yourself onto drugs or something that gives you that false sense of security. In saying that, I don't think this sort of information should send all parents into a panic. Y'know, 'Oh my God! My child has an eating disorder.' No way! I think it's more a case of remembering, we gave the child the right to expression, therefore we gave the child the right to be and to feel. So in return we must be prepared and willing to listen and respect, and I'm not so sure we are.

I'm getting to the stage where I'm thinking, damn eating disorders, damn alcoholism, damn whichever label that you want to attach. Damn these avenues, 'cos we're talking *compulsive addictive behaviour*. It represents a *dis-ease* with ourselves, for whatever reason, and unless we start looking at this whole other umbrella, we're going to get so channelled into looking for the symptoms of an eating disorder that we miss the fact that it's already taken root.

Working towards recovery

I think the most important thing for professionals encountering anorexics is to remember that they don't want to tell you. They don't want you to know (this, of course, in the cases where the problem is detected, as opposed to being told about it by the sufferers(s)). An anorexic is a professional liar and you've found them out. It's no use giving them information out of the newspaper or something. They'll just hide unwanted food, and maybe laxative packaging with it, and bin it!

Reflect back on what you've observed, and identify – empathise – with those feelings of isolation. Instead of starting a sentence with, 'You are doing something wrong' say, 'It must be horrible to be lonely.' Encourage the person to open up. If you confront someone on the attack – 'You must be anorexic' – they'll back off, whilst if you confront the situation empathically you stand a better chance. If there's no reaction to that then, yes, you may have to go in with both feet. You see, it's all about choice and making the person aware they have a choice. That there are better ways to cope. That there are better friends.

Remember, recovery comes from being desperate enough rather than wanting it, and it is about learning to re-experience feelings. If you wake up feeling shitty, you just experience it. People with eating disorders are trying to solve it. They're trying to stop their feelings, and/or deny them. All the feelings they were trying to starve away are gonna resurface and they've got to learn to cope with them. As I stressed earlier, thin means not feeling fat, which to an anorexic and bulimic symbolises anything above their current weight, means refeeling, and it's agony. Everybody needs to know and understand that the recovery process can't happen overnight. Unlearning bad habits is a hell of a procedure, and learning constructive ways of coping is painstakingly difficult. It is a process, so therefore recovery takes commitment. You need to know what's involved.

Reference

Cox, A. (1995) *Autumn Dawn: Triumph over Eating Disorders*, Sussex: Book Guild.

Ann Cox
Interview by Daren Garratt
The Open University

9

Young People and AIDS

The Dudley HIV and AIDS Support Group present an account here of their work with young people. It focuses on the support they give to those with HIV and explores their wider work in schools and the community.

Our work at Dudley HIV and AIDS Support Group covers everything from preventive work to work with a small client base. We support people with HIV and have a hardship fund which people with HIV can access. We also put together training programmes for our own volunteers, as well as providing HIV education training for other groups.

We actively go out to women's refuges, colleges and schools, and we've recently worked with year 10 pupils, who are aged between 14 and 15. In the training sessions we try not to concentrate too much on the roots of transmission and the biological aspects of HIV. What we talk about is *attitudes* more than anything. You find with 14 and 15 year olds there's quite a bit of homophobia which we expect when we go into schools. We don't go in thinking everyone's 'right on' or pc [politically correct]: we challenge existing attitudes. That's what we're there for – to challenge. We get everyone talking about attitudes to HIV, and it gets very loud and vocal. People do get het-up about it, but, y'know, if you can actually bring these things up to the surface, that's better than just sitting there and lecturing people.

Notions of 'high risk' groups

I don't know if young people still view HIV/AIDS in terms of 'high risk' groups or not. It's very difficult to gauge because, obviously, there's been a lot of media coverage and political correctness going on . . . People are loath to stand up and go, 'Ooh, it's the gay plague', but really, deep down I think that attitude still prevails. On the whole, though, I should say most young people do have a good grip. They know the facts that it's no longer a specifically gay, drug-based epidemic, but getting *them* to take on board that *they* could be at risk is more difficult. You still get the 'I don't like condoms' mentality with the blokes, and if anyone's got any ideas how to get over *that* one I'd really like to hear it!

We try and educate with games and illustrations 'cos they're enjoyable to do and that surprises people. Sometimes you can actually see the information going in!

The National Curriculum and Section 28

The National Curriculum *is* a problem, 'cos it seems they can't fit us in anywhere. The schedule's so tight anyway y'know, it's difficult to go in and even do two-hour sessions. Really we could do with going in and doing two hours per week for a number of weeks in order to cover everything and really get into the subject, but obviously schools don't have that sort of space in their agenda. We tend to be given a two-hour spot at the end of an assignment, but ideally, what we'd like is for HIV education to be integrated into all training patterns.

Now Section 28 is a different matter. There's a lot of scare-mongering about the legislation and people like ourselves going into schools and doing training. What the Local Government Act 1988 actually says is that you can't *promote* homosexuality, but we're obviously *not* promoting homosexuality. We're promoting safe sex and AIDS awareness. Obviously, when we go into a classroom we ask for a teacher to be present simply because of the content of what we're talking about.

We're not allowed to answer individual questions! So if a kid asks a question you have to say, 'Well look, I can't answer that so go home and ask your mum!' That's why we ask for a teacher to be in the room, so if anyone *does* go home and ask their mum there's no comeback on us. We have to know we're covered in what we're saying, 'cos there's also this thing called 'the corruption of innocents'. I mean, you're talking about 14 and 15 year olds here! Now I'm not saying *all* of them, but a significant number of this age group are sexually active, and they are all sexually aware. I can't see how we're 'corrupting their innocence' if we're giving them information that could possibly one day save their lives.

Also, it's difficult to get back into the schools and see what effect you've had. I don't know if they do specific follow-up work, 'cos as I said earlier, the training's incorporated into a wider topic anyway. I think some schools *do* carry on and work with the knowledge we've brought in, but it's still very early days for us as a group. There are also problems with us being a voluntary organisation, as there seems to be a credibility gap between the statutory and voluntary sectors.

Young people

We don't ask people's ages when they phone, unless they sound really young, but we do get all ages contacting us. A nurse actually rang the other week and said, if a 10 year old phoned us and asked advice, would we give it? And we *would* give advice, but it would be geared to that child's level of understanding. Y'know, we wouldn't start talking about safe sex practices to a 10 year old! But if they had a specific question about HIV infection that they may have heard, then we would try and clear that up, but at a level that a 10 year old would understand.

Because AIDS affects and concerns everyone, age doesn't really make a difference. It's easy to sit back and say the older generation aren't concerned or interested in HIV, but they are actually. It does seem to be trendy to be *into* AIDS at the moment, though. Did you notice all those celebrities wearing red ribbons during World AIDS Week? I couldn't help but wonder how many of them *really* knew what it meant.

Changing attitudes

In 1985 or 1986 the government had the 'Don't Die of Ignorance' campaign and the warning that 'By 1992 everyone will know someone who has died of AIDS' . . . well, of course it didn't happen. Whether it was because of heightened awareness, the success of the campaign or whatever . . . it wasn't the massive epidemic that was predicted. And it lulled people into a false sense of security. Unfortunately the number of people being infected is slowly creeping up again, but it's really difficult to draw the line between informing people and scaring the shit out of them, and that's the thing you have to consider when talking to young people. You can try and frighten people, but all they'll do is shut off 'cos that's the normal human reaction. It's really tempting to say, 'My God! Do you really want this to happen to *you*?', but you can't. You'll achieve nothing.

Another problem is that most people still think of AIDS as being a superstar disease. They still think you have to sleep with an incredible amount of people and do lots of bizarre things, when in reality it's people like me and you who get it.

Regional figures

'Figures' are what people ask us for most, but we really place no importance on them. They're not reliable. We could spout figures left, right and centre, but we'd be manipulating them and would therefore be lying. What's the good in that? Regional figures are distorted anyway, but for social reasons. We've found that if you find you're HIV+ in a small provincial town, what do you do? You've got no support system available to you, no services, you can't tell anyone, you've got no community, no acceptance . . . so you just leave. Go to London and become one of their 'figures'. And that's happening all over the country.

But being HIV+ doesn't have to be a death sentence. It may be easy for me to say, not being HIV+, but if you've got a lot of support it is possible to live a fulfilling life with HIV, and that's what we want for all the people we come into contact with. There's a crucial difference between referring to someone *living with* HIV or AIDS, and someone *dying from* HIV or AIDS.

Coping

It's one thing learning about HIV, but then seeing someone who has been debilitated by the virus is a whole different ball game. In a way it can put your whole reason for wanting to do the work back into perspective. But of course, at times it can be very stressful work. Y'know, some nights I'll go home after a really traumatic day, pick the kids up from school and get inundated with all these questions and gripes and you just want to *scream!*

But we do have supervision and support systems for all the volunteers and workers. We have access to counsellors and everybody supports each other within the group.

Suzanne
Dudley HIV and AIDS Support Group

Interview by Daren Garratt
The Open University

10

Exploring Homelessness:
the Young Person's Viewpoint

*Here two young people describe their experiences of 'life on
the streets'. The young people concerned were interviewed at a
project for young homeless people in the West End of London.
London Connection undertakes work that actively seeks to
support homeless young people. The project is concerned to
offer health, welfare, social, education and training opportunities. It also provides daytime shelter and subsidised meals.
'J.' is a young man who has lived on the streets since the age
of 15. 'M.' is a young woman who has recently left home after
experiencing physical abuse by her father.*

Ending up on the streets

J.: I originally came from West London. I went into care at the
age of 11. I started absconding when I was 15 and that's how
basically I come on the streets; run away from Essex to
London and started sleeping rough from then. In and out of
hostels but mainly on the streets; sleeping bags; blankets;
anywhere where you can just get cover for the night.

My mum was a drug addict, she was a dealer, basically she
couldn't cope. So I had to go into care. I was slapped on with
a seven-year care order.

I started absconding because it all started getting to me.
First of all I didn't know what was happening, then all of a
sudden I clicked on what was happening, and in four years I'd
had enough. It was like a prison sentence. Just counting the
years as they go by. It felt like wherever they threw my
suitcase I was there really. I had no choice in the matter or
say where I wanted to live.

M.: Well, firstly I left home because of domestic violence. My
father was beating me. It wasn't just the physical side of it. It
was also mentally disturbing as well being at home. I left
because of that reason and I'm still studying which is really
hard at the moment. I wanted to leave home since before

GCSEs but I didn't know what was on offer for me basically. So I just stayed there as long as I could. Then two weeks ago on a Friday my dad beat me severely and that's when I decided to leave home and I said I wasn't going back.

I'd had a social worker involved with me before I left home. But she said that basically I don't need any help from her at the moment. So I'm going alone. She said that because I was in full-time education and had got my head on my shoulders that basically she doesn't really need to help me. And she said if I've got any worries I can always go and see her. She's given me a phone number to ring her whenever, and I go and see her once in a while to tell her what's going on.

Living on the streets

J.: I was born in London and living in Kent. I missed London because all my family was there. As they say it was the 'bright lights' that bring you to it. I thought it was a change to see what London was really like for myself. And to tell you the truth I hate it now.

My first experience I can remember was, it was a cold wet day, I didn't know where I was. First night I found myself sleeping on the Strand in a doorway. I was kicked, spat on because I was sleeping rough in the doorway. I actually met someone who helped me get blankets and showed me what it was like. I didn't sleep that night because I didn't know what would happen. I'd heard so many bad things about it that I was really scared.

From there I went into my first hostel. That reminded me of being back in the children's home. I came out of there and went back onto the streets. And then stayed rough. And then I found London Connection and I've used it for the last three years.

I've had to sleep in dirty doorways; people chuck all their litter over you. Generally they think you're a bit of 'scum'. I never thought I was going to be in this situation.

M.: When incidents with my father happened I left home and I stayed at my friend's house. I was also walking on the streets; staying in flats; in the corridors of flats. Living with a friend? Well you can't really rely on your friend to look after you all of the time. She has got her own family. You can't expect your friend's parents to support you. I was there a few days and I left; walked the streets a bit. I was on the streets for a few days. It was cold. I felt really isolated and a bit vulnerable as well. I stayed in the park a few times. Got scared that my wallet would get nicked. Also, there is the possibility of getting raped and stuff like that. It never came down to that though. You just feel really scared because you don't know what's going to happen.

A woman is more vulnerable on the streets because of all the hassles from guys, and not really knowing what to do. I suppose you feel weaker as well, because you know that a guy could easily be stronger than you. You do get scared of guys coming up to you and stealing your wallet, pressuring you into doing things you don't want to, and there is also a lot of drugs going round as well. I think if you're vulnerable you could be led into prostitution very easily. You get guys coming up to you, especially in the Soho area, but you've just got to make sure you know what you're doing. I've had offers of people saying 'will you work for us?', but I've always turned it down. People who get caught up in prostitution, I think it is financially because they haven't got enough help. So that's the only thing they can really get into.

Support on the streets

J.: You get to know each other and you all look out for each other. If there's trouble with the police or anything like that you go along and help them. You're like a big family, you stick together, and when help is needed it'll be there.

Before I come on the streets I had some support from the social services. But once I turned 18 that was it. The care order was off and as far as they were concerned you weren't in their care no more. You were on your own basically. We'll chuck you in a little flat and you survive, goodbye!

Since I've been on the streets I had help from street workers and the advice team from the Connection. The street workers come round the streets looking at homeless people; telling them about day centres; where they can get hostels; free food, blankets; the general stuff you need when you're living on the streets. They are someone to talk to, if you need someone to talk to. They are there to listen. They go out of a night-time and mainly visit round the West End. Some kids on the streets take their advice and some don't. You sit there and listen but at the end of the day you've got to make the decision to take their advice or not.

London Connection

J.: London Connection is a day centre for kids between ages 16 and 25. They have an advice team that help you with housing, get your ID like social security and birth certificates. They have work space where you can look for jobs. They have a computer room where you can do examinations and apply for jobs. They have a drugs advice team that come in once a week. There's a doctor and an optician that comes in. You can do sports. Basically there are lots of people who come in to help get young people back together.

The project helps you with [the] Rough Sleepers [Initiative]; I've actually got a flat off them. So once I got that I could get a job. They are helping me look for work. Basically they have helped me get my life together. Help is always there if you need it. They have always got time for you, and you just come in and use the place.

Interviews by Stanley Tucker
The Open University

11

Someone to Care: the Experiences
of Young Carers in the Community

Caring for someone who is sick or infirm can be a difficult task. In Britain it is estimated that around 200,000 young people play a significant caring role within their families (Becker and Aldridge, 1994). They look after parents, grandparents, brothers and sisters, aunts and uncles etc. They carry out tasks that require them to administer medication, undertake a physical and emotional caring role, as well as support other family members. The accounts that follow are an amalgamation of the views expressed by eight young carers who were asked to discuss their day-to-day experiences (extracts of young people's views taken from Liddiard and Tucker, 1996).

The experience of caring

The experience of caring can produce both positive and negative feelings. Often, those young people involved find themselves questioning their role and family relationships.

Why me?
> The only thing that ever went through my mind was, why me? Why my family? Why not somebody else's? But I sort of got over that. I used to get very very angry. I wanted to be like a normal family.
> I think the worst thing is seeing someone you love, someone active that becomes tired of walking. They can't walk down the shops, they have problems getting in and out of the bath and can't go outside. That's what gets to you more than having to do things. It's more a case of seeing someone who was so independent and now knowing that they can't do it, that hurts. But then I think you're in a situation like this, you'll just have to learn to get on with it and cope and do things, and just hope for the best really.
> I get angry, not with her for being ill, but angry with others for not making an effort; because she still worries the house isn't tidy enough. My brothers for example, I think I get really angry because they won't tidy up. They just won't make an effort and she just says, 'Oh they're only young.' And I say, 'Yes, but you know I have to do it.' My dad says to them they should do it, but really he can't enforce it. He works

shifts. He works all night, so he sleeps most of the day. As they come home from school he's just going out, so they don't tend to take much notice of him.

You always try not to make her worry, because making her worry doesn't do her any good. So I suppose you're more careful about things and you tend to do more for the family.

Oh beautiful child

Yet, it would be wrong to characterise the lives of young carers as being full of 'doom' and 'gloom'.

It's enjoyable in some ways, because I get to do lots of things I like. I like the cooking. It's nice if there is a mess or something and you clean it up and you think, I've done that well.

She can be really happy sometimes. That depends if something's happened like when she goes out. That's my time when I do all the housework and everything. She comes back and she's saying, 'Oh beautiful child.' I look at some 16 year olds and think they seem really childish, because how they act and everything and I've never really been like that.

Not many people I know can like do this stuff. My friends don't really know how to work the washing machine, they can't cook, but I know that I can do all these things. You learn as you go, you know. Yes, you are scared sometimes thinking you won't be able to cope. But you are really happy when you achieve new things. It's like that for me all the time.

The caring day

She's usually so tired then she'll sit down and do nothing

Caring responsibilities for some young people continue even when the person they are supporting is on the 'road to recovery'.

Well she's actually back to work now. She's not as bad as she was. She has to take a lot of time off, but most days she goes in so she starts early. I get my brothers up, make sure they're wearing their uniforms, that kind of thing. David will go to school without his tie and he knows he's going to get into trouble, so we get letters home and that just stresses everyone out and yet he still does it. So I have to make sure he has got his tie with him. I have to make sure they have got their money and that they've made their lunch, and this, that and the other, and I'll get them packed off. Then my friends knock for me and I'll go to school leaving the house relatively tidy. My mum works about two or three hours. She gets back about eleven and she's usually so tired then she'll sit down and do nothing. On most days I get home about four, half past, and then I'll start housework and sometimes she helps me.

Most of the time I start at the top and work down and then they get home and mess it up again!

I have to do things like, if there are appointments to be made, I'll make them. I handle Phil's football team and all that, anything that needs to be done. Everything has to be paid for. I mean, I don't financially support them, but I have to arrange the money. She's getting better. She's taking a lot of the responsibility back, but before everything was down to me.

Trying to get everyone in at the same time is a bit of a disaster in our house. They don't want to be in; there's always one out here and one there, so I round them all up for dinner and they eat and then usually me and my mum will clear up the kitchen between us and she'll go back and sit down and I'll get on with whatever needs doing – homework or schoolwork.

Being on hand: it can mean a long day
The caring day sometimes places heavy physical and mental demands on young carers.

Yes, in the morning I help my dad – sometimes at night as well, because he's in pain or wants to get out of bed. My mum can't do it, she's ill herself, so he calls out and either me or my brother go and come down and help him. It's all the time really apart from when I am at work. So it starts from after work until I go to work in the morning. Sometimes he can have a good day and doesn't need any help getting up. On other days it will be every quarter of an hour: getting him out of the chair, or making sure he stays in the chair; to calm him down; to give him a drink; hopefully make sure he takes his tablets; help feed him his dinner if he can't do it; and just general things like that.

I get up about five o'clock and have my bath. Then about seven wake her up, give her something to eat, get her clothes out for her, and if she wants anything else, do it for her. I get ready for school about quarter to eight. I do the housework because my dad he's really tired. I cook him some dinner and stuff like that. I'm coping with the night-time and he's coping with the day.

And what about support and free time?

Meeting the demands of both home and school, and finding space for leisure, is a difficult balancing act that many young carers perform on a daily basis. In some families support is readily available, whilst in others it is not. Friends and neighbours can also provide much-needed assistance, and yet it appears many health and social welfare professionals still find it difficult to specifically recognise the needs of young carers.

I needed to get out

She goes to bed at half past eight, nine o'clock and so do they [her brothers] as well. So I'd go out then, which wasn't such a good idea when I think about it, staying out late and getting up early. But I needed to get out and have a bit of a break. I got into trouble while she was ill. I think because of the stress. I needed an outlook. I just got in with some bad lads; kept it all a secret, you know. I mean I didn't do anything really stupid, but they were all older than me and I knew my mum and dad wouldn't like it. I kept it a secret and got found out, as you do.

I went out last night with a friend just to do two hours' shopping and I was something like 15 minutes late. She was so worried 'cos I wasn't back on time. That kind of makes it that every time you go out, you're thinking I've got to get home. I can go out if I want to, but I know I worry when I'm away as well.

When dad gets up, he's got an hour to two hours before he goes out, and so I go out. On Saturday is my day.

Families, friends and neighbours

We live quite close to my grandparents and mum's one of six children actually. I felt they could do so much more. They could come and see her, but nobody does. Unless she went to them, she didn't see anyone. I resent them even now, my grandparents. Well I've got no time for them any more.

I've got two brothers, one's married, the other one's separated and they've got their own families. They've both got young children so they are not about as much as me and my sister. I mean we see them. They come over and visit and things like that. They ask if we need anything. They don't really think as much as me and Lou do about things.

Because my dad sleeps during the day we've got the next door neighbour and she's really pally with her. She comes in during the day. On a weekend she has all her friends in. They gather round so it gives me a chance to go out and they have a chit-chat.

Yes she comes in and like sits with him and she calms him down and she helps make sure he's in his chair and everything. Well it gives my mum and me a break, but my mum doesn't really get a chance to go out by herself. There has always got to be someone constantly looking after my dad. Because Judith's got a child of her own, she can't come over for a couple of hours while my mum goes out.

Professional support

The nurse comes in and she makes sure my nan's alright, I think about once a week. I'm in school when she comes. We've had no help from social services. We was going to have a home help but I said I could do it.

My dad's social worker, she doesn't speak to me or my brother about how we feel about caring for my dad and what we've got to do. She talks to my mum but she only says about putting my dad into a home.

She doesn't say, how are you getting on? Or, how are things looking? Or, are you OK about caring for him? Or, are your son and daughter alright? No, it's about putting him in a home all the time, and my mum doesn't want that.

Yet, recognition of the young carer's role can help to produce a more positive response to the situation.

I got consulted on it a lot, because every time there was a meeting or something to be discussed, my social worker arranged for me to be there; for like after school; have time off school; the school knowing about it; things like that. We had a big meeting about four weeks before Christmas and I had about an hour off school to actually attend the meeting. There was the doctor, the nurse that comes in during the day, and there was several other people, my social worker, me and my mum, my grandad. I think we are well catered for now.

Understanding the needs of young carers

Young carers have very specific needs that are pertinent to their particular situation. However, they also appear to have a range of shared needs:

Having someone to talk to in a similar situation:

If you're with a group of you, you know you're not the only one in the same situation.

Having someone to listen to their problems:

I think that would help people, especially young people, because I've never had to look after anyone before.

Having someone there to support you while you support someone else is probably nicer.

Receiving support services that were more appropriate to their needs:

I need a break from it. She [the father's social worker] doesn't like give us any counselling about looking after him, which is pretty bad, I think.

Becoming better informed and more involved in decision-making processes:

Just being noticed and listened to, that would be a start.

Having access to appropriate financial support:

I don't think carers are financially supported very well, and young carers are mostly ignored.

References

Becker, S. and Aldridge, J. (1994) 'The price of caring', *Community Care*, 20 January, pp. 18–19.

Liddiard, P. and Tucker, S. (1996) *Milton Keynes Young Carers Project: a Pilot Study Looking at the Experiences of Caring of Eight Young People in Milton Keynes*, School of Health and Social Welfare, Open University, Milton Keynes.

Penny Liddiard and
Stanley Tucker
The Open University

12

School Exclusion: a Different Response?

The issue of school exclusion is one that has attracted increasing public and political attention. Here a teacher working on an NCH Action for Children school exclusion project talks about her concerns for excluded young people and her work philosophy and practice. NCH Action for Children is a national charity that supports work with children, young people and their families.

There's a built-in failure

Over many years I've worked with kids who have been persistent truants, in trouble with the law, or excluded from their secondary school. However, what worries me enormously is the increased level of exclusion we are now witnessing in schools throughout the country. In some ways I think the increase was inevitable when we decided to have league tables and individual tests that would rate performance in a very narrow sense. You are going to get certain children and young people who senior school staff do not see as advantageous to the school. In a way they are not cost effective in terms of the staffing and effort their needs demand. It is understandable that concern often has to be with the 'greater good'. Difficult youngsters take time and effort in terms of dealing with their behavioural problems and chasing them up for truanting, or following up awkward and sometimes violent incidents. And they don't bring kudos to the school in terms of their academic achievements.

Now, it is easy to decry these young people, many of whom have had really bad educational experiences, but we have to realise their needs are different and very individual. They don't always fit neatly into a school setting, and they can't always easily cope with the demands made on them by school. In some ways they are set up to fail: there's built-in failure in the large and often unwelcoming structures of the secondary school. It often starts when they are quite young and it just gets increasingly worse.

There is a certain amount of containment in schools. There are young people who are just about being held onto but not really educated. The ones I work with are those for whom the situation has completely broken down. There are a large number of youngsters floating around in the system receiving only a minimum in terms of home tuition and support.

Developing work with excluded young people

For me there are some important ideas that have to underpin work with excluded young people. First, young people need to be cared for and respected as individuals. All young people should be treated in this way, but for excluded young people this is particularly important. Next, they have to come to a project, like the one I work on, because they see some real value in attending. This will be different from their normal experience in many cases: it has to be recognised that the undisciplined pupil is not missed in school, and their absence may be welcomed by hard-pressed teachers. That is understandable from a discipline point of view, but it does little in terms of motivation. You have to want young people to stay if you are going to work with them effectively. In many ways that's the bottom line.

After that, young people have to have a clear sense of why they are on a project. The important thing is to work together and create meaningful personal objectives. Objectives that should be regularly reviewed. Objectives that will give a sense of purpose, so that they can say, 'By the time I leave I should have achieved this, this and this.' I also think you need to develop very clear ideas about sanctions and incentives. This helps to create proper working boundaries. Everyone knows where they are. We have to work out between us what is acceptable behaviour and how behaviour that doesn't fit in will be responded to. Now, I accept this can be difficult for young people who have had bad educational experiences, but we can't shy away from it. It isn't helpful in terms of preparation for later life.

A sense of self-worth

There is a need to work with excluded young people and help them improve their self-identity and give them a sense of self-worth. There is a need to help them find a sense of direction. Within that, part of my role is to help them get some sort of piece of paper that they can wave at prospective employers and colleges. But also to improve their basic skills: literacy and numeracy are really important here. The majority of youngsters I work with, due to their educational history, well, their educational levels tend to be very low, and in fact they can all do far better than they are doing now. Alongside that I need them to recognise what their problems and shortcomings are for themselves. So many come to the project with the feeling that what they do is rubbish – without any real value or worth to anyone let alone themselves. And they almost, therefore, give up before they have started. You have to go step by step so that they actually come to realise they can achieve things. I try to get them to a point where they say, 'Yes I can.'

What kind of curriculum needs to be available?

The curriculum on offer needs to avoid being too generalised. You cannot just set one piece of work and hope that everyone will do it. Individually negotiated packages of learning are all-important. It is also important right at the beginning to undertake some kind of screening and test out where each of the young people are at. Screening in terms of what we can find out about individual ability levels, confidence, communication skills and general strengths and weaknesses. This then helps to create a baseline to work from. It has to be recognised that young people work at different paces, even if they are struggling with the same kinds of problems and ideas. You can then get an educational package together that responds to individual need as well as their basic skills.

Exams are also important for many excluded young people, even though they may think it is far too late. Here, the important thing to remember is that a variety of exams exist, AEB, City and Guilds etc., that are flexible. Crucially they are also seen to be of value by employers. We've got to get away from saying it has to be this or that exam in an absolute sense. I also welcome National Vocational Qualifications (NVQs) and their workplace focus. I'd like to make more use of these kinds of qualifications as they develop. I know schools are already thinking and working towards this. It can only be helpful in the long run.

On a day-to-day basis you have to work in ways that are non-threatening and will give plenty of opportunities for achievement. I tend to use group and individual exercises and worksheets. You have to give time to settling the group each time you work with them and allow them to talk about where they are at. I spend a great deal of time on the basics: maths, English through written work, dictation and reading, and life skills. It's a matter of creating variation as far as possible but working to an identified core that everybody recognises is important.

Information technology (IT) should also play a real role in work with excluded young people. There is a whole host of software available to support individual learning, and the Internet is still relatively untapped. The potential of this learning resource is massive. Learning can be supported, but mistakes made on the privacy of your own screen. The skills are also transferable and will make the individual more employable in the future.

Projects also need external advisory support from their local education authority. It is important that the individual project does not become a 'dumping ground' left to its own devices. After all, if excluded young people were still in mainstream or special provision, advisory support would be made available to their teachers. The situation should not be different because they are out of school. I need to be exposed to new thinking and ideas. It is important not to be marginalised and to be able to obtain ongoing training. All of that will help me to continually improve the curriculum available.

Further education and work placements

There is a real chance when young people are excluded that they will become isolated from their peers. Small groups and projects can also serve to exacerbate the problem. Therefore, it is important to prepare young people for work placements and the possibility of further education (FE). In the longer term we all have to fit in and live in groups. But you can't push anyone forward before they are ready. Again, I return to the importance of individual work and preparation here. Careers advice becomes all the more important, as well as selecting the right kind of work placement where they have a real chance of fitting in.

FE is only a runner when the young person has a chance of obtaining support in the college itself. You have to remember that self-esteem is often low. In a way, they will expect to fail again. I'm really pleased that more and more colleges are now working in the area of special needs support. If this is done sensitively, and in a way that responds to individual need, this can only be helpful.

Lois
Interview by Stanley Tucker
The Open University

13

Passing Time? A Story of Community Service

In the account that follows a young man talks about his experiences of community service. He recently received 120 hours for stealing from cars. The interview was carried out when he was age 19 and in the middle of serving his sentence.

More than being bored

What I'm going to talk about is fairly ordinary, it happens to loads of kids like me all over the country and most of my mates have been through it as well. It's life where I live. You get caught up in stupid behaviour early on and it grows. I'm on it [community service] now more or less as the last resort before being sent down. People tell me it's a chance to change and be different, but I ain't sure about that. Yeah, I'll do my hours and get on with what I'm told to do, but to think it's like going to mean much more – well it is and it isn't. The staff are fair and some of them that supervise you are really good, you can talk to them and have a laugh. But at the end of the day you know why you're on community service and that's right that you should.

In a way I think I always thought it would come to something like this. Nicking cars, stealing cars; helping yourself to bits out of them, radios, mobiles, cash, anything you can sell on; that's how it is. You don't think about who owns it, you just go for it. Sometimes you can be walking down the road and the window goes in, or we plan it, go out to steal on the car parks where the shoppers are. Mostly you do that kind of thing for cash, but it's more than being bored. People should try being out of work. It's hopeless when there aren't the jobs round here, and as my old man says there won't be the jobs again. Anyone listening to me might say it's like that for loads of people and they don't steal. Yeah, I agree with that to a certain extent, but we're not all the same. Like I'm not perfect and sometimes I take a chance and go for it because, well, there isn't any other way of getting the cash.

When you actually nick cars that's a bit different. You're just buzzing from start to finish. You're with your mates and everyone you think is chasing you. Stupid really because lots of times you don't even get noticed and you dump it on a road and walk off. But I've been in chases and that's something else. The danger? You think about it a bit, but it's like so noisy in the car, screaming and shouting at each other, music full on, all that stuff. You say do this and do that – it's a bit like on the telly except it's for real.

Community service: it ain't soft

Last time I got 120 hours when I went to court. The magistrate gave me a right bollocking, said all the stuff about this is your last chance and if you don't change then it will be prison. I'd admit now I was a bit scared, 'cos basically there's always a chance of being sent down. Yes, I was glad to get out of that place in one piece. But afterwards you like forget most of that stuff pretty quickly and make a joke about it with your mates. I wasn't the same bloke in the pub the night after!

The first thing about community service is it takes your time away, and 'do I not like that' as that idiot we once had managing England said. You've got to turn up regularly otherwise you're what they called breached and it's back to court. Someone sits down with you and works the hours out, but in the end you've got to give up your time – weekends, nights – until it's all finished. This is one of the big things that gets to everyone on it [community service], even if you're sitting around or waiting in a van, because it's raining or something like that and you can't cut grass. It's just someone saying to you, be there or else there'll be big trouble.

Some people think it's easy on community service, like you don't really do much. Most of them that thinks like that have never been anywhere near it. I been working on this community centre, it's near to where I live but not on the same estate. Really run down it is. Some group runs it, they have no money to do anything and there's this one old woman who just goes on and on about how the council wouldn't give them anything. So I guess we're like filling in for the council. We had to paint the outside, it was absolutely rotten. It had to be scraped and then the wood filled and then it was ready to paint. I remember coming back once and some little kids had been pissing about with the paint, I went really mad. Not just about the kids but because these centre volunteers, as they call themselves, had let them do it. Sounds stupid in a way, but like it seemed to me someone was saying it's only the community service lot, it doesn't really matter. But in the end we like had no choice, we had to get on with it and clean the walls off again.

I want to say something about the supervisor we have called Reg. He's absolutely great. You can have a laugh and a joke, but he's firm as well. What I like about him is that he gives you a job to do and then lets you get on with it. He's been in the building trade for most of his life, so he actually knows what he's talking about. But he'll show you things. He's got loads of patience and everything. I wish someone like him was in school when I was there, because you need people to help you like that. The other thing about him, he's not always on your case, saying things like why did you do this, steal cars, thieve, stuff like that. He'll talk to you about down the pub, and home, and everything. We've had some absolutely brilliant conversations about City and United. He's a City fan but that's OK. What I know is he's not like those crappy social workers, always going on about things they know nothing about. Yeah, I know what you say about trying to help. Some of them are not too bad, but some just want to interfere all the time – it's not on.

What have I learnt?

Like I was saying to you before, I've learnt absolutely loads off Reg. Practical things, but useful for later I suppose. I don't want to make a long list; spending time with someone who'll help you is the thing. Not putting them down if they don't do it first time. I've learnt what I don't like doing as well. Grass cutting and cleaning up rubbish, someone else's shit, what's the point of that? It's the same again the next day. There's been plenty of that; that's the punishment bit.

You learn to play the system pretty quick. When to keep your head down, who to mix with, what will get you in trouble and what won't. How far you can push things with some chaps. You listen to what other people have done, or what they say they've done. I ignore a lot of it, most is bullshit, talking up the big 'I am'. Some of them get believed though by the others and they act like heroes. There are chaps on the scheme who need to be brought down a peg or two. I've seen Reg do that, make them look soft, but they still think they are the king. I suppose they'd be like that wherever they were. Me, I'm a distance away from that, I've seen it all before and done a bit myself.

Yes, there are positive things about doing it [community service]. But it's not the push-over you might think. It has made me think about if stealing and robbing is worth it. I'm not saying I won't get caught up again, chances are I probably might. But at least I could have a few second thoughts, especially when you know that the next thing is going to be prison. I don't want everyone to think that I'm reformed because of what I've said. You've got to carry on living in your area and all that goes with it. What would change me? A proper job, not schemes and all that crap, no, a real job with proper money to spend on a Friday night down the pub. Basically you would feel a bit more like everyone else.

Perhaps the one thing I could do here was to give a message to all those who want to lock people away all the time. Community service, if it does nothing else, gives you a bit of space to breathe and think about things. You might meet a half-decent bloke like Reg on the way who I think really wants to help. You need people like that, real people who tell it like it is and actually know what you are talking about.

Adrian
Interview by Stanley Tucker
The Open University

PART 2
GETTING A LIFE

Projects

14
Home from Home

The Young Single Homeless Project is based in Dudley in the West Midlands. It is a local authority funded initiative that seeks to provide personal support whilst meeting the accommodation needs of homeless young people or those leaving care. Here the project co-ordinator talks about the work involved and some of the issues and problems that young people face in moving to independent living.

About the work

Each young person is assigned a member of staff as a key worker, and the day-to-day business of the project mainly consists of the young people coming in, having a chat and talking about any issues or things that concern them. We will then offer our support and help to them to sort out any particular problems they may have. On top of this there's additional time within the week where the key worker will sit down with the young person, go through various bits of paperwork, and generally see how they're getting on. We also assist with the development of practical skills. We supply the opportunity to do cooking, and if the young people have never done their own washing, there are the facilities to show them how to do that. Basically, we try and assess what stage of development each young person is at when they come in, what skills *they* think they need to acquire, and what skills *we* think they might need if they are to successfully move on to independent living.

Skills and considerations

I think the most important skills required for this type of work are to be aware, and sensitive to the situations that young people find themselves in. It really is hard for them out there, and it's not getting any easier. Everytime there's a budget, or there's some new legislation, if it's going to have a negative effect on anybody it'll be young people who feel it the most. And in some ways, whilst we can stabilise that situation to a certain degree, let's face it: if you're on a low income, you're on a low income. That is a hard reality of life they have to quickly face.

One thing we can do is get them to look for work or training that as far as possible reflects their skills and abilities – even when the job market is really limited. And although they've been through a process of adjustment, in that they have got their own accommodation, the story doesn't end there. It's part of the solution that they've got a permanent roof over their head, but there's all the other issues that then present themselves. The one that keeps recurring for us, and that we try to keep in mind, is that when a young person moves out of hostel-type accommodation or has been homeless, they can then apply for a community care grant. Now, that's all well and good, and it's fine that they've got access to that, but they can't actually put the claim through until they've got a permanent address. The problem then is that there's a delay of something like four to six weeks before that grant is paid. So unless that young person has had the forethought to gather up bits of furniture or pots and pans, and has had them stored somewhere, they're faced with the prospect of moving into a new, generally unfurnished flat, and they'll not have the finances to equip it. Then there's the situation where if they're on a low income, they might be able to claim some benefit, but again, there's a delay while that claim's being processed as well.

Housing benefit

All the time we encourage them to balance their budgets. After housing benefit have taken their share there's not much left. But it still has to be managed. We try and get them to put money to one side for food, clothing, things like that. Sometimes if they haven't really managed money before we have to keep a close eye on them. So it's not that all of a sudden they've got to find this unexpected rent as well as everything else that they will need to live on. It's not an easy task for lots of young people. A couple have been quite 'cute' and managed to get the housing giro issued directly to them, and all they've done is built up huge arrears, which they may not be concerned about at the moment, but should they want to get a council flat they'll have to pay that off. That can be another learning experience!

Location and relocation

Because we don't take people directly into the project, they have to go to the Housing Advice section of the local authority and are interviewed there. Then, once they are identified as being legitimately homeless, they have a number of options, which include ourselves. So, it doesn't necessarily mean that if a young person turns up homeless at Housing Advice they'll automatically come here. We might argue they ought to come here, but it's the housing department's responsibility. They send who they want to send.

Sometimes other organisations will ring us up and ask if we've got space for someone who's just turned to them looking for help. Where we can, we like to say yes, but in the end Housing Advice act as the filter.

The other main issue we face is about numbers. There's a lot of homelessness 'out there', and yet we go through periods where we've got really low numbers, which is mystifying. The only conclusion we can draw, and we have discussed it with a number of other organisations, is that the market's changing a bit now. Young people are saying, 'Yes, we're homeless, but we don't want just anything.' They want smaller set-ups, 'cos there's maybe a stigma about coming into a project full of homeless people. Perhaps they want something a little less obvious – smaller flats of two or three people. Of course, if that was the set-up we could still go in there and work the way we are now.

The other message we're picking up is that people don't necessarily want to travel. We've found that a lot of young people want to stay in their local communities where they know people, and they can stay in touch with their friends. And at the end of the day, is that too much to ask?

There's not enough temporary accommodation for young people *where they want it*. The transition to independent living can be greatly assisted if you have got your peers around you. You need people you can turn to when the going gets rough. In part, that's what the worker does – he or she is there when the going gets tough. But we're also talking about a process of social education here – building life skills, confidence, exploring options.

You don't learn these kinds of things by 'osmosis'. We have to create opportunities for young people to make mistakes so that in the end they will move forward.

Neale Pilkington
Young Single Homeless Project, Dudley

Interview by Daren Garratt
The Open University

15

Learning on a Saturday:

a Case Study of an African Caribbean Supplementary School

Cheryl Gore is a researcher at Birmingham University who also teaches at a supplementary school for African Caribbean children. The following is a case study of this school.

Inequalities in the mainstream education system

African Caribbean parents and others within the African Caribbean population have long been concerned about the low levels of educational achievement of African Caribbean children. The move to establish supplementary (Saturday) schooling arose out of this concern. Not only have British schools been consistently failing African Caribbean pupils, but African Caribbean people in this country have also found themselves in a position in which they have been forced to defend themselves against racist theories which attributed their children's failure to either culture or biology.

The findings of several studies (for example, Rutter et al., 1979; Smith and Tomlinson, 1989; Nuttall and Goldstein, 1989) suggest that which school a child attends plays a much greater role in determining achievement in public examinations than his or her ethnic origin. Inner city schools, for example, tend to achieve much lower results on average than schools in other areas. This is a significant factor in the 'underachievement' debate as certain minority ethnic groups, including people of African Caribbean origin, reside predominantly in inner city areas. Inner city schools and other schools with a predominantly working class intake had a history of underachievement long before there were substantial numbers of black pupils attending them. In fact, prior to concern with 'black underachievement', debate in Britain centred around working class underachievement.

Differences in the socio-economic composition of different black ethnic groups correspond with the differences in educational achievement between different black ethnic groups (Jones, 1993). Since areas of residence and consequently the school attended are related to social class, this relationship between class and achievement appears to support the proposed relationship between the school attended and academic achievement.

Establishing the school

The African Caribbean Saturday school which is to be the focus of this chapter is located in inner city Birmingham. There are approximately five other such schools in the local area; and at the time of writing there are nine African Caribbean supplementary schools in Birmingham in total. As far as I know, to date none of these schools has received any form of funding. Section 11 funds have been used to finance supplementary schools in the past (Stone, 1981). However, in recent years there have been cuts made in the funding which is allocated to local projects. Supplementary schools of this type in Birmingham are unlikely to receive such funds as the local authority does not appear to be in favour of supplementary schooling.

The study Saturday school was set up by an African Caribbean worker at the community centre at which the Saturday school is held. He said that he decided to set up the school because he had seen children in the area grow up without achieving much academically; and he saw poor education as the main reason that African Caribbean people in this country are not generally successful.

He started by assembling a committee, which consisted of interested African Caribbean professionals and community workers. The next step taken was to advertise for teachers for the Saturday school by sending posters and letters to local schools. This initiative did not receive any response. Letters were also given out to parents of pupils of all ethnicities in local schools. However it was clear from the letter that the proposed supplementary school was to be aimed at African Caribbean children. These letters received a good response. Enquiries were also made into obtaining a grant. At this stage however the committee members withdrew owing to pressures on their time.

At this point in time there were three people who were willing to teach; and parents who were waiting to send their children to the school. The worker who had initiated the project thought therefore that it would be best to launch the school, despite the facts that at this point there was no management committee and the school had no funding. The school therefore began in December 1994, a year and half after the first moves to set it up had been made.

The philosophy of the school

The philosophy behind the supplementary Saturday school is similar to that of many others (Chevannes, 1979; Clark, 1982; Stone, 1981; Tomlinson, 1984). That is, the main aim was to attempt to tackle the problem of low academic achievement of African Caribbean children, brought about primarily by structural inequalities within the British education system. Another aim of the Saturday school was to redress, to some extent, the still predominantly Eurocentric curriculum in mainstream schools, by including within the Saturday school curriculum African and Caribbean history and geography, and educating the pupils about people of African descent who have made important contributions in the past. The Saturday school staff also hope that having African Caribbean teachers at the school will provide role models for the children. It is also important for African Caribbean children to have teachers who do not hold negative stereotypical views of them in the way that some teachers in mainstream schools might.

In addition, the fact that the children attend a predominantly African Caribbean school on Saturdays, it is hoped, will help the children to have a more positive self-identity, and greater self-esteem. The school provides a safe environment where the children will not be victims of racist abuse as they may be in mainstream schools. The area in which the Saturday school is located is ethnically mixed. Most of the pupils at the Saturday school live in, and therefore attend mainstream schools within, the local area. However one pupil who does not live in the local area gave the fact that there are more African Caribbean children at the Saturday school as the reason he preferred the Saturday school to his weekday school. Therefore, at the very least, the school provides the pupils with a setting in which they can be with other African Caribbean children.

The school in operation

The curriculum at the Saturday school consists of maths, English, and African and Caribbean history and geography. The children are also taught about the achievements and history of people of African descent in the USA and of people of African and Asian descent in Britain. The pupils are taught maths and English as the staff believe that it is essential for the children to be equipped with the basic skills which they will need if they are to succeed within the British education system.

The teaching is carried out using a variety of methods. The pupils pay a minimal fee of one pound each per week, and this money has been used to purchase textbooks and stationery supplies for the school. Some of the maths and English textbooks which have been bought are Caribbean textbooks, which therefore include references to Caribbean countries, foods and customs. A few books concentrating on black history have also been purchased for the school. Pupils typically during maths or English lessons either work from exercises photocopied from textbooks or are given work set by the teachers themselves, such as spelling or multiplication tests, mathematical problems, or English assignments such as essays or letter writing.

Black history is taught in various ways. Pupils may, for example, be asked to read about a famous black person and then complete a comprehension exercise about that individual. Occasionally pupils are asked to copy the picture of a famous black person from a book and write a few important facts about them underneath. Alternatively pupils may re-enact an event in history or the life of a famous black person, working in small groups. African and Caribbean geography are taught with the use of maps and information regarding the population and economy of the individual countries. Pupils are encouraged to draw upon any personal experiences they may have from visiting countries in the Caribbean or Africa.

Recently links have been forged with another Saturday school in the local area. It is hoped that the staff at the two schools will be able to support each other, by sharing ideas, skills, knowledge and resources. It is also hoped that the pupils at the two schools will benefit from interacting with each other. Recently pupils from the other Saturday school have joined pupils from the study Saturday school on two occasions: for a quiz, and for a Christmas party.

Conclusion

This therefore is how the school is operating at present. There are certain difficulties. For example the lack of funding. At present the school still has no source of funding (other than the minimal fee which the pupils pay to attend). No applications for funding have been made as yet, although application forms for applying to the local authority have been acquired. It is the intention of those involved in the operation of the school to get African Caribbean headteachers of local schools and African Caribbean education researchers to write letters in support of the school's application for funding. No advances have been made with this initiative as yet owing to time constraints.

Another possible obstacle which may lie in the path of the school's progress is that the community centre which accommodates the school has been threatened with closure. It should however be possible to locate alternative premises in which to hold the school.

Nevertheless the school has many positive aspects. The children enjoy attending the school; and the implicit message which is conveyed to the pupils by the very existence of the school is that their parents and the Saturday school staff (who give up valuable time to work at the school, without payment) are concerned about their education. The implication here is that the wider African Caribbean population also believes education to be of great importance.

The impact of the 'message', the basic academic skills and black history which the children are taught, the presence of teachers of African descent, and an environment which is predominantly African Caribbean should all have positive effects on the children who attend the Saturday school. That is, it is hoped that the Saturday school will not only lay the foundations for academic success, by ensuring that pupils have mastered basic skills, but also encourage pupils to retain their high aspirations throughout the secondary schooling which they will soon encounter. Knowing that a majority of African Caribbean people have a high regard for education; being taught by African Caribbean teachers; and being made aware of the achievements and history of black people (and specifically of people of African descent) from a non-Eurocentric perspective, should give the pupils both the resources and the determination to succeed within a society in which they suffer from both racism and social class inequalities.

References

Chevannes, M. (1979) 'The Black Arrow Supplementary School Project', *The Social Science Teacher*, 8 (4): 136–7.

Clark, N. (1982) 'Datchwyng Saturday School', in A. Ohri, B. Manning and P. Curno (eds), *Community Work and Racism*, London: Routledge and Kegan Paul.

Jones, T. (1993) *Britain's Ethnic Minorities*, London: Policy Studies Institute.

Nuttall, D. and Goldstein, H. (1989) 'Differential school effectiveness', *International Journal of Educational Research*, 13: 769–76.

Rutter, M., Maughan, B., Mortimore, P., Ouston, J. and Smith, A. (1979) *Fifteen Thousand Hours*, Somerset: Open Books.

Smith, D.J. and Tomlinson, S. (1989) *The School Effect*, London: Policy Studies Institute.

Stone, M. (1981) *The Education of the Black Child in Britain*, London: Fontana.

Tomlinson, S. (1984) 'Supplementary and segregated schooling', in S. Tomlinson (ed.), *Home and School in Multicultural Britain*, London: Batsford.

Cheryl Gore
Department of Cultural Studies and Sociology
University of Birmingham

16

Cascade Peer Education Drugs Programme

The Cascade project works in the field of drugs education with young people. Here the aims of the project are examined and an overview is given of work carried out in schools, youth groups and colleges.

Overview

Cascade was established in 1992. Funded for an initial period of three years by the Home Office Central Drugs Prevention Unit, the programme was established to develop peer-led drug and substance education for young people aged 11–21. The main areas for delivery of the programme were schools, youth clubs and colleges but it was anticipated that there would be a range of venues in which the work could be tested.

Cascade is a Crime Concern project. Crime Concern is a national organisation that provides consultancy and training in the field of community safety and crime reduction. In 1991 Crime Concern undertook independent research in the borough of Solihull in the West Midlands with 250 young people in schools and youth clubs. This research drew attention to the concerns that many young people have about drugs and drug use and also that the then current methods of drugs education were not addressing the issue in a manner seen as relevant to most young people. The research also concluded that from the age of 14 years, many young people preferred to talk to, and get their information from, other young people and, in the main, tended to be distrustful of adults who shared a different drug education agenda.

Location

Solihull is situated in the West Midlands conurbation bordering the city of Birmingham. The total population of the borough is approximately 200,000. A major road runs across the middle of the borough (the A45), and in effect presents a dividing line in terms of wealth and class. To the north of the A45 Solihull is generally urban with a large Birmingham overspill estate called

Chelmsley Wood. This area has the highest level of deprivation, unemployment, health problems and crime.

South of the A45 is the town of Solihull together with several small towns and villages. This area is rural and wealthy. In the centre of the borough lies Birmingham Airport and the National Exhibition Centre; both are large employers. The variety of locations provided by Solihull has been important in considering the methods for delivering a peer education strategy that takes into account urban and rural locations and the different needs that may arise from them.

Aims and objectives

Cascade was funded by the Home Office to test out the possibility of developing peer-to-peer methods of drug education.

The objectives of Cascade are:

1 to develop a peer-led drug education strategy for young people aged up to 23;
2 to influence the drug and substances policies and practice of key local agencies, particularly education, social services and criminal justice;
3 to develop a work programme and materials that can easily be replicated both locally and nationally.

In 1995 an additional objective was added: to take into account the need for support for parents and teachers.

Methods

Cascade is primarily concerned with providing quality drug education and awareness for young people, parents and professionals. The project is concerned with primary prevention and harm reduction including basic counselling and support. We do not provide any clinical or rehabilitation services.

The project relies heavily on young volunteers to undertake its work programmes. Currently the age span of volunteers is from 14 to 23 years.

Cascade encourages all young people in Solihull to become involved. There is no selection procedure and we recognise that some of our volunteers are themselves 'users' and have a range of experiences regarding drug use. All training and support is provided free of charge and involves the following areas:

1   knowledge about drugs and substances;
2   the law and legal issues;
3   attitudes and values in relation to drug use and users;
4   harm reduction;
5   further sources of help – what other agencies can do;
6   planning workshops and other activities;
7   monitoring and evaluation.

The training programme is flexible and makes use of residentials, day events etc. The programme is geared to the age and ability of participants. We make much use of active learning methods and the training workshop structure is designed to facilitate the development of *knowledge*, explore *attitudes* and build social *skills* and confidence.

Emphasis is placed on providing the information that young people require in an accurate and unbiased way. In line with current UK thinking we have not adopted a 'say no to drugs' approach. Instead Cascade volunteers encourage other young people to make their own informed choice based on the facts. Cascade also recognises that many young people do not see their drug use as problematic, even though they are breaking the law, and in this context we need to be pragmatic and ensure that young people have the necessary information that allows them to 'keep safe' and reduce potential harm.

Work with schools

Cascade volunteers running workshops in schools find that it is easier and more effective to work with classes at least one year younger than themselves. Volunteers work in a team of not less than two. Teachers are encouraged *not to remain* in the classroom in order to allow for confidentiality and also to reinforce the 'peer-to-peer' nature of the workshop. The methods used involve 'active learning techniques' such as quizzes, games and role-playing. The key aim for a school workshop is to raise awareness, create debate and provide the first four elements of the list detailed above. One of the problems with school-based work is that the time allocated for running programmes is very limited.

Other school-based approaches developed by volunteers involve 'drop-in' information points, roadshows that tour school sites at lunch-times, questionnaires and special projects, which can include drama, and art and design work.

Youth clubs

This work is very much the same as above but is less formal and geared to the more fluid nature of youth clubs.

Colleges

College-based work involves workshops, the provision of information and advice points, organised debates and social events. The work tends to be focused towards established 'users' and as a result the range of materials used in the peer programmes is more controversial in its nature and content.

Materials

Cascade makes use of materials that have been developed by other agencies. We have also developed materials relevant to our own locality. This is important because local youth culture needs to be reflected through leaflets etc. Young people are currently developing their own materials for use amongst their peer networks.

Research

Cascade recognises that for many young people their drug use is not seen as a problem and they would not consider discussing their recreational drug use with a doctor. Thus recreational drug use is not reported. We have been carrying out our own confidential research with young people in Solihull to establish what drugs they are using, frequency of use, their knowledge of drugs and the associated risks, and attitudes to drugs and drug use.

Cascade has reached over 7,000 young people since January 1993 and trained and supported over 150 young people as volunteers.

Cascade, Solihull

17

Youth Choices: Bridging the Gap

Young people moving towards independent living are faced with a bewildering range of decisions. Some of the choices they have to make can have significant consequences for both their immediate and longer-term futures. But for many young people the options for housing, employment, education and training are limited by their social and economic circumstances. These young people may need assistance in bridging the gap between life at home and living independently.

Identifying the need

A significant minority of 16 and 17 year olds are not participating in any form of education, employment or training. Many are not in contact with any agencies which might offer assistance or direct them to constructive activity. Each month about 12,000 people aged 16 and 17 apply for severe hardship payments, a benefit intended to be a last resort for young people in need. Accommodation is a major concern for many.

Many of these young people will effectively be excluded from mainstream society and isolated from possible sources of help and support. NACRO (the National Association for the Care and Resettlement of Offenders) has long been concerned with helping people reintegrate into the community and to make the most of their potential. Clearly, for many of these young people, traditional routes through education and training to employment are not suitable or appealing and other factors affect their ability to participate in and benefit from such opportunities. Specialised programmes are needed which can respond to a range of needs, and attract and engage disadvantaged and disaffected young people and enable them to rejoin society.

A question of choice

Youth Choices is just such a programme. Initially piloted in Northumbria, the programme developed from concerns about those 16 and 17 year olds who were 'missing' from education, employment and training. By seeking young people out on their 'territory' – outreach work in pubs and clubs, shopping centres and parks – the project was able to identify what was preventing them from taking up opportunities to learn or to find work. The programme helped them consider their skills and interests, try out a variety of training opportunities and consider realistic options, in a supportive environment. Local agencies were involved in the establishment of the programme and in its delivery; the network of joint working arrangements included youth centres, young offender institutions, probation services, social services, courts, intermediate treatment centres, special schools, drug and alcohol projects and housing departments.

A training programme was established, based on existing initial training programmes (designed for those young people who might otherwise be unprepared for mainstream training owing to: low motivation; needing further assessment or assistance with choosing a vocational course; lacking basic communication, literacy and numeracy skills; or other special needs). The programme addresses training needs and offers training 'tasters' in a number of vocational areas whilst also developing personal skills and interests.

Over 200 young people were contacted by the project during the first year. As a result of this contact, 88 took up youth training. The participants in the programme came from varied backgrounds and experiences. However, there was a heavy over-representation from care leavers, those recently discharged from custody, others who had been involved in the criminal justice system, and yet others who had previously been persistent school non-attenders or had learning difficulties.

A significant finding during the first phase of Youth Choices was that, of the 200 participants, 80 were homeless. One of the major recommendations of the first project was, therefore, that training in life skills and home management be included in special needs training programmes where participants had recently begun living independently or were homeless. Without an address, it is difficult to claim benefits, almost impossible to get a job, and hard to avoid resorting to crime. An especially debilitating consequence may be an inability to organise daily living, with very low priority being placed on longer-term commitments such as training and adapting to the world of work.

As well as decent, secure and affordable housing, many people also need some support and practical help to live independently. Responsibility for rent, bills and budgeting for everyday living expenses, may well have seemed insuperable barriers to maintaining a tenancy. A failed attempt to live independently can, in turn, increase feelings of isolation and exclusion. Reintegration into the community, the world of work, training or continued education, and the move to independent living need to be encouraged through the provision of appropriate support and assistance.

Improved choices

Youth Choices II offered a package combining vocational training with skills needed to live independently. As with the first Youth Choices project, the project's development process included consultation with the young people themselves, establishing their needs, barriers to getting assistance, gaps in knowledge and ambitions.

The course covered areas such as welfare rights and benefits; basic home maintenance; budgeting; diet, nutrition and basic cookery skills; rights and responsibilities as a tenant; personal and domestic hygiene; and health education. The Youth Choices courses were designed to be delivered on a rolling basis which would allow trainees to start and finish as their needs dictated. They were practically based and the balance between life and training for work skills varied according to individual needs, as did the overall length of the initial training period.

Staff made direct contact with 112 young people. All were in temporary accommodation, were homeless or needed additional support to maintain their tenancy. Participants were assisted in moving from temporary to permanent accommodation. Others were helped to register as homeless to determine their priority for local authority housing; some returned home after a 'cooling off' period between them and their parents. Project workers obtained clothing for some tenants, helped with form filling and encouraged them to follow up options. Many of the participants appreciated the befriending role project staff took, helping them overcome feelings of loneliness and isolation. They particularly welcomed staff coming with them on visits to other agencies.

Most participants progressed to mainstream youth training, others went into further education or training for work (for those over 18) and some obtained employment. Several gained word-power and numberpower foundation level certificates and one completed an NVQ level I in information technology. All of the young people finishing the programme received certificates of attendance and achievement. Staff were able to intervene to prevent a number of trainees dropping out of training at the onset of homelessness. A high proportion of Youth Choices clients were ex-offenders. Staff were able to use their experience in working with ex-offenders to give constructive practical advice on resettlement.

Onwards and upwards

Following the success of the first Youth Choices programme, NACRO has been able to establish similar schemes in a number of areas across England and Wales. These programmes have attracted funding from training and enterprise councils (TECs) and other sources, including local authorities and the European Commission, to offer young people access to programmes which are co-operative and integrated, and that facilitate flexible approaches between relevant agencies in responding to young people's need for help with training and employment.

Certain key factors contribute to the effectiveness of the Youth Choices model when working with young people facing multiple disadvantages. These include:

1 a friendly and informal supportive training environment;
2 staff with skills and expertise in working with troubled young people;
3 a flexible approach to training, offering modules to suit individual needs;
4 time built into the training programme to allow for personal development;
5 strong co-operation with local agencies in designing and delivering courses and providing referrals and offering additional assistance;
6 vocational training 'taster opportunities' to allow participants to make informed choices about appropriate and appealing forms of training;
7 access to initial and basic skills training.

The flexibility of the programme makes it easily adaptable to meet the needs of different target groups. NACRO has run a similar programme working specifically with young Asian and black people, who are particularly disadvantaged and under-represented in the labour market and training field. Another offers vocational guidance, support and counselling, as well as training opportunities, to young women who are pregnant or have dependent children. The programme has been modified yet again to work with very young people who are not attending school regularly and may benefit from exploring training options earlier than usual.

The value of Youth Choices is clear. It provides a cost effective and successful way of bringing young people into the labour market whilst attaching them to mainstream society.

I love Youth Choices. It's great. I like the attitude of the staff, they're down-to-earth and treat you like a human being. We talk about drugs, benefits, safe sex. You can talk to all the staff about anything and they'll help you. You get really good advice. During the 12-week course you are helped to decide what you want to do and draw up an action plan . . . I wish it was longer. I've made friends. Before I was pretty lonely. (Clare, aged 17)

NACRO, London

18

Advocacy

Here Jane Dalrymple, the director of Advocacy Services for Children, explains why advocacy work with young people is so important.

> Once you know what your rights are you've got your little piece of soil on which you stand. You're not just a free floating subject . . . You're somebody who has to be listened to.
>
> M. Berlins, 'The justice diary of Albie Sachs'

Albie Sachs, talking about the concept of a society based on rights, strongly believes in the South African Constitution, which is based not on granting rights to people but on people having rights which cannot be interfered with. When we are considering rights in relation to children and young people it is important to remember this principle. What does this mean to children and young people experiencing the law as it affects their lives? Does the law give young people rights which are respected and recognised? Are their wishes and feelings taken into consideration when decisions are made concerning their lives? Are they empowered?

In trying to answer some of these questions I will consider how to promote anti-oppressive practice in relation to working with children and young people and some of the barriers that both adults and young people experience in practice. This will first mean reflecting on the power relations that exist between adults and young people. I will then consider the process of advocacy as a means of anti-oppressive practice and the dilemmas practitioners may face in this role. Finally I will look at ways of promoting a culture of advocacy.

Childhood

Many people do not like to use the word 'oppression' in relation to children and young people. It is not a comfortable word. But until adults recognise that they can and do oppress children and young people it is not possible to promote change. At a workshop about controlling challenging behaviour I was once accused of denying young people the right to childhood. This belief about childhood is one which is socially constructed. Freeman (1983) points out that the concept of childhood varies culturally and historically and the division between 'adult' and 'child' is one which is both arbitrary and incoherent. If one looks at the various ages at which young people are deemed to be 'adult' it is easy to see that the notion of what is acceptable 'adult' activity is confused and the product of 'historical accidents and responses to particular pressures at particular times'. All adults will have a view then about children and childhood – from considering children as property to viewing them as potential adults. However, Malfrid Grude Flekkoy (1991) reminds us that children are rarely considered by adults as individuals with special but equal value as human beings. She goes on to state that 'even when they are considered as "equal", they may still not get the respect for their dignity and integrity which is accorded to adults' (1991: 217).

Children and young people generally are a powerless group of people in the adult world and have consistently been denied full rights to participation by those with power – adults. 'Adultism' then can be seen to be the oppression of children and young people by adults. There are alternative words that could be used to describe this oppression. 'Youthism' has been used to express the same notion. Whilst strictly speaking this is probably a more correct use of language, I consider that the term 'adultism' more forcefully states the power differential that exists between adults and young people.

In order to be able to exercise their rights, children and young people always rely on adults to some degree. They are often the recipients of 'decisions' made by adults 'in their best interests'. Young people can be oppressed by decision makers: by adults who are professionals and often take control, and by those who are policy makers who decide on service provision.

Promoting anti-oppressive practice

In order to combat adultism it is necessary first to recognise that the oppression of young people occurs at two levels: individual and institutional. Having recognised that a power imbalance exists, anti-oppressive practice is then about trying to promote change to redress the balance of power. In order to do that we need to

1   understand the mechanisms that result in young people being denied access to resources and thus feeling powerless;

2   try to provide the means by which individual young people can regain control of their lives (Dalrymple and Burke, 1995: 18).

There are however a number of barriers that adults put up to deny young people their rights and so maintain control. As David Hodgson observes, 'genuine confusion and anxiety about children's rights are easily exploited when adults feel their own entitlements to be under threat' (1994: 25).

It is important to recognise that in order to promote change in the provision of services for children and young people, three things are needed:

1   We need a commitment to understanding how organisations can and do oppress young people.
2   We need to rethink the relationship between the organisations in which we work and young people for whom services are being provided.
3   We need to take responsibility for ending that oppression.

Accessible services

Recent research into the provision of youth information, advice and counselling services identified some key characteristics as important in making a service accessible to young people. Whilst I am not discussing how to make services generally accessible to young people, if we consider these characteristics we can see how powerless young people feel if such factors are not present when they have contact with adults, particularly professionals.

The characteristics identified as key are:

1   self-referral facilities;
2   confidentiality;
3   informality in approach and style;
4   perceived as independent by the young people;
5   specific to young people;
6   a generalist approach.

Of these, the elements of confidentiality, informality and independence together with a generalist approach were identified by the young people in the research as being crucial to a positive service.

For many children and young people who are in receipt of social care services the important decisions in their lives are made by adults, usually professional adults. They are often made in adult initiated meetings such as reviews, case conferences and planning meetings. The young person should be a part of these decision-making processes. But there is an increasing body of research

(Barford and Wattam, 1989; Dolphin Project, 1993) which suggests that young people find them daunting and adult focused. In fact they are often daunting for the adults as well. Nigel was an able and articulate 14 year old young man who went into local authority care after his parents separated. He understood the importance of going to the meetings but never felt included: his experience was that he was there to be viewed. His frustration and unhappiness about what was happening in his life evidenced itself in behaviour which adults found unacceptable and he stopped going to school. He contacted an independent advocate to support him in the meetings. His advocate's first experience of a review was exactly as Nigel had predicted. The adults spent much of the time discussing Nigel's behaviour and 'telling him off'. He became upset and ran out of the room before the meeting ended, confirming the adults' concerns about his difficult behaviour.

What happens if a young person disagrees with the outcome of the meeting, or has not been involved in the process or consulted? Well legally there is provision for young people to make a formal complaint to the social services department. This is a great step forward in terms of legal rights for young people to seek redress for poor service delivery. However it is often difficult for young people to complain about services, particularly if they fear retribution or withdrawal of the service. It is even more difficult for young people who already feel disempowered, and who do not feel that they are valued or respected. Robina complained about the way she was treated in a children's home and felt that she was subsequently labelled as a 'troublemaker'. She found it difficult to continue, even with the support of an adult advocate, for fear that the labels would be written in her file and make her life in care more difficult.

Young people who find themselves in receipt of social care services, whether in social services care, residential schools, hospital wards or other day service provision, need to have access to someone who will listen and support them so that their wishes and feelings can be taken into account and their voices heard. However such a service needs to take into account the characteristics outlined above identified by young people as being important to them to make a service accessible.

Advocacy services for children and young people

One way of helping children and young people to have a voice is through the provision of an independent advocacy service. In May 1992 a service providing advice, advocacy and representation for children and young people (Advocacy Services for Children, ASC) was set up to help those children and young people who are defined as 'in need' under the Children Act 1989. The aims of the organisation are to ensure that children and young people have a voice when adults are making decisions about their lives. It does this by empowering them to use the services offered to them by social care agencies in ways which ensure maximum benefit to their self-esteem and overall development. It is informed by principles which respect the rights of children and young people as enshrined in policy and legislation as well as international instruments such as the United Nations Convention on the Rights of the Child.

ASC consists of a team of independent advocates who offer a confidential service to children and young people who feel that they are not being heard. Young people can contact an advocate either through a freephone helpline or by using a freepost contact card. All the advocates are adults who are carefully recruited from professionals who work in child care related fields. You may wonder whether young people might find such adults intimidating. However the rationale is very simple. Young people are not listened to by adults. Adults will listen to other adults. And adult professionals listen to other professionals. It is a sad fact but true. That being the case it is sensible to support young people by ensuring that those who act as their advocates are competent and able to do the job. All professionals should use advocacy as part of their repertoire of skills in working with young people. But to function properly an advocate must be independent.

Advocacy work with children and young people is not easy and it is the experience of ASC advocates that they frequently have to explain their position. It is therefore often even more difficult for social care practitioners to advocate on behalf of a young person against their employers, even if they believe that the wishes and feelings of the young person are valid. Social workers can respond to young people and practise from an empowerment perspective, but it is difficult if the perceived 'best interests' are not in line with the young person's wishes and feelings. It can be argued, of course, that if the wishes and feelings of the young person are ignored, and if they are not involved in the decision-making process, then their best interests are not being considered.

Even trying to set up a young persons' panel to inform the work of ASC has been an uphill struggle. As part of our commitment to being young person focused and therefore involving young people in every aspect of the organisation – interviewing, training, policy making etc. – we have a young persons' panel which meets regularly. However, adults are constantly putting barriers in the way. It is not seen that young people have a right to participate, or that it can help improve their social skills! Joanne was representing ASC at a conference in London. Her ticket had been bought. Accommodation arranged. She was to be accompanied by an adult. At the last minute her carers decided it would be unsettling for her as she was due to move to a new placement the following week. Joanne was not consulted about this decision – merely informed.

Many professionals struggle with balancing the dilemmas that appear to exist between ensuring that decisions are made in the best interests of children and young people and ensuring that their wishes and feelings are taken into account. Judith Timms (1995), however, points out that 'it may not always be that the local authority view and the best interests of the child are one and the same thing, although there is a prevailing fantasy to that effect which manifests itself in the assertion that any contradiction of the local authority view is, by definition, failing to give consideration to the welfare of the child.' She goes on to state the following advantages in involving young people in future planning:

1   Involving children in decision making increases their sense of identity and self-esteem.
2   If children have been involved in the making of a decision, they have a sense of 'ownership' and an emotional investment in positive outcomes, which means that plans are more likely to succeed.
3   Even if consultation does not lead to the outcome the child would have preferred, participation in the decision-making process can still leave the child with positive feelings.
4   It is possible to allow children and young people to have an input into the decision-making process without burdening them with the responsibility for making the decision.
5   The young person's perspective may encourage adults, or agencies, to think more flexibly or consider a wider range of alternatives.

I well remember a young person who told his advocate that the guardian *ad litem* had not put forward his views correctly. She had written what he actually said, but then followed it with an interpretation of what she thought he meant. He meant what he had said! And as the expert about himself, he believed that his views about his situation were in his best interests.

References

Barford, R. and Wattam, C. (1989) 'Children's participation in decision making', *Flachee*, 5 (2).

Berlins, M. (1995) 'The justice diary of Albie Sachs', *The Guardian*, 11 July.

Dalrymple, J. and Burke, B. (1995) *Anti-Oppressive Practice and the Law*, Milton Keynes: Open University Press.

Dolphin Project (1993) *Young People Answering Back*, Southampton: Southampton University.

Flekkoy, M.G. (1991) *A Voice for Children: Speaking Out as their Ombudsman*, London: Jessica Kingsley.

Freeman, M.D.A. (1983) *The Rights and Wrongs of Children*, London: Pinter.

Hodgson, D. (1994) 'Right on', *Community Care*, 10 March.

Timms, J.E. (1995) *Children's Representation: a Practitioner's Guide*, London: Sweet and Maxwell.

Jane Dalrymple
Advocacy Services for Children

19

Direct Action! Positive Responses to Crime

How can young people respond to the issue of crime in their communities? Crime Concern is an organisation that is concerned with developing the social, educational and personal skills of the young, so that they can work together to respond to local needs and priorities.

Identifying a need

Crime is perceived to be a problem of the young, and with 45% of recorded crime being committed by young people under the age of 21 there is some evidence to substantiate this perspective. It is often too easily forgotten that young people are also the main victims of crime, especially violent crime, which is committed, in the main, by young men against other young men. For many young people their concerns about crime commence when they are the victims of the 'hidden' crime often occurring at school. In this environment, bullies can reign, racial harassment is common, property is vandalised and stolen and drugs are trafficked.

Like the rest of society, individual young people feel powerless to counter such infringements on their lives. However, when a number with similar concerns come together they find that they can change things. Peer group pressure can be used in a positive way to inform others how to counter being a victim or even influence others not to become perpetrators. Young people are likely to become empowered to take some action when:

1 They have experienced being a victim.
2 They are supported by a concerned adult who understands how to enable them to achieve their objectives.
3 They have the information and resources to stimulate solutions to problems.
4 They have had some success, received acclaim and seek higher goals to achieve.

Crime Concern, the national crime prevention agency, with the financial support of the Prudential, staged conferences for young people to express their concerns, surveyed young people's attitudes to identify their issues, and produced resources to provide guidance. By the end of 1995 over 1,000 youth action groups, involving some 20,000 young people, were being offered support by Crime Concern and the Prudential to play a part in countering crime and improving safety. This account reviews some aspects of that work.

Turning concern into action

No blueprint is available to cover all local circumstances, but Crime Concern is driven by a belief that by empowering young people as partners against crime, longer-term solutions will be achieved. Across the country a number of ways of working with young people have been developed. These include:

1   The use of police school liaison officers to work in partnership with teachers, often with responsibility for social education and citizenship. This approach gives value to the activity through the school curriculum.
2   Area crime prevention panels which focus on work with youth, making it a priority to develop youth crime prevention groups.
3   Youth workers and youth organisations focusing on aspects of good citizenship as a feature of their activities and achieving results that receive community acclaim for their members.

The approaches used included:

1   bringing together groups of young people with a common interest;
2   letting young people take the lead, set the agenda and its priorities;
3   enabling young people to develop a number of solutions that could be put into practice
4   ensuring that the processes used were fun;
5   enabling the young people involved to tell their story to the press and media;
6   creating circumstances where young people could receive the credit for their achievements and be given value and acclaim for their contribution to a milestone passed or goal achieved;
7   using a 'snowball' approach that applies the previous principles to a growing range of issues.

A sense of being

Citizenship can easily be dismissed and misinterpreted as a topic about how society operates. To make it come alive young people need to be given responsibility for taking action on issues that affect their lives and the lives of others for whom they have some collective responsibility. The law and under-age drinking can easily become a peer group survey and a study of the consequences of a 'problem'. Citizenship is concerned with playing a part in society but more important it means the valuing of young people's contribution and giving it recognition. For example, some young women surveyed their town and identified all the areas where they did not feel safe and they presented their findings to the local council. As a result many of their recommendations were acted upon. That's empowerment.

What are the benefits of involving young people in citizenship issues?

1   They develop an increased awareness of issues affecting society.
2   They feel safer, are less afraid of crime and are less likely to commit crime.
3   Their relationships with the police, teachers, youth workers, and representatives of other agencies improve.
4   They find out that learning about tackling serious issues can be enjoyable and rewarding.
5   Taking action improves their self-esteem, confidence, self-discipline and ability to present their arguments, and creates a feeling of responsibility.

A case study of action taken by Salisbury School action group, Enfield

Salisbury School action group was set up by deputy head Sally Waugh and local school liaison officer PC Robin Clayden in the spring of 1994.

As part of a school council project an interested group of six young people met together who were concerned about the image of young people and the impact of crime on their lives. Their first task was to agree on a name for the group and design its logo. As they were concerned about stopping problems around the school they became known as Salisbury School Clampdown.

To involve the rest of the school in deciding what the real issues for young people were the group obtained two old ballot boxes from Enfield Electoral Registration Office and located them around the school for suggestions. The group examined the issues that came forward and voted on them to establish priorities, and then the group's chair and a colleague took them to the school head for his approval to take action. The whole school was informed of the group's proposals for change through school assemblies and parents through the school's newsletter.

The initial project was to deter vandalism and the group approached the head with the idea that he should give them a vandalism budget. Every time damage was done the group would lose money from their budget. Any savings at the end of the year would go to the group. In the first year they replaced the lower school drinking fountain. To deter graffiti in the upper school girls' toilets senior female students went on toilet duty. Initial success has led to the idea that the girls should redecorate the toilets in a decor of their choosing.

Members of Clampdown take action to counter aggression in the school and students will get involved if they see incidents that they feel are unjust. A recent 'mugging' outside the school led to information being disclosed and further action being taken. Some students no longer feel that this is 'grassing' on the culprits but consider that it is giving assistance to the victim.

To counter litter a referendum has been staged and as a result the lower school has been declared a litter-free zone. A further referendum ensured that cans are recycled as a positive way of improving the environment. An anti-bullying campaign was also developed in the early part of 1995 and a confidential drop-in centre was located in the lower school, later to become known as Speakeasy. To change the group's motivated concern for others into helpful counselling skills, Victim Support staff came into the school and trained Clampdown members.

The original group of six is now some 30 strong and can list a whole new range of skills they have gained, including chairing meetings, negotiating with senior staff, writing reports for governors and parents, and evaluating the success of their projects for applications to such bodies as the Business and Industry partnership. Members of the group now make presentations in local primary schools and promote Salisbury as a safe school in which to learn. Students previously referred to within the school as difficult students with aggressive and volatile behavioural characteristics have changed their behaviour and supported staff and other students when supervising others. The previous chair of Clampdown has recently obtained employment with the local council and this she attributes to the confidence and skills learnt through the group's activities.

It is early days in the life of the group but already they have seen how they can make a difference to the lives of others within the school community. Contacts with Victim Support, the Office of Fair Trading and Neighbourhood Watch are beginning to demonstrate how Clampdown members can play a positive role in the wider community. After two years of operation each success has led on to a greater one.

Partners in crime

Working through schools is not the only way of creating young people as partners. Other agencies can also play a part:

1   In the Thanet area of Kent, the social services youth opportunities team had developed a safe school policy to counter drugs, truancy and child abuse in local secondary schools. However they considered that young people should and could play a part in making schools safer through the youth action concept. With the assistance of a local project worker, 11 secondary schools in Thanet now have youth action groups which are supported by an inter-agency group.
2   Kingston youth service, as part of its policy of empowering young people, supported a group of young people wishing to stage their own conference on crime issues. The enterprise of the young people attracted the local Rotary club to offer financial and practical support to ensure the conference on young people's crime concerns took place and continues to take place on an annual basis.
3   The Weald of Kent crime prevention panels, inspired by what had been achieved by youth action groups in London, launched their own initiative which involved supporting young people with conferences, drama workshops and training for teachers and police officers on how to empower and lead from behind.

All over Great Britain various partnerships have been formed to provide the backing structure to youth action. The core funding by the Prudential has acted as leverage for partner sponsorship at local level. Education officers and local council crime reduction programmes have provided further support. Crime prevention has been recognised as not the sole preserve of the police. Just as significant is the part that young people can play through a range of peer-led activities which are increasingly being recognised as an integral part of local community safety strategies.

Alan Bailey
Crime Concern

20

Bullying: Mediating a Response

Lucy Griffiths, a headteacher in a West Midlands school, talks about the importance of peer-mediation as a way of reducing incidences of bullying in schools.

You get it for being Jewish
Get it for being black
Get it for being chicken
Get it for fighting back
You get it for being big and fat
Get it for being small
O those who get it get it and get it
For any damn thing at all.

Adrian Mitchell, 'Back in the playground'

Dear Childline,

There is this girl who always teases me and provokes me and I hate it. I hang around with a large group of people and she is one of these people. It sounds strange but it's true. When she does this my other friends just laugh and I pretend to laugh but I feel like crying. She has never hurt me physically but I think mentally is worse. Sometimes when I go home I cry. I cry so hard. I really don't want to be friends with any of them any more but I don't think any one else would want to be my friend and anyway some people in my group are nice. I don't tell my mum or sister (I don't live with my dad) because I would be embarrassed and I really could not tell them it would make matters worse. Please could you write back and tell me what to do but disguise the letter so my mum does not find out.

(letter to Childline from a bullied young person)

Bullying like becomes a way of life. Hitting out at anyone and everyone is something I've always had to do. When you been pushed around like me, well in a way your copying what's happened to you. I'm strong, I won't deny that, and bullying always gets a reaction. But I want to say that not only people like me bully. I've been the victim of bullying by adults. You know those teachers who stand up full in your face and bawl at you. Staff in the homes where I've lived who make you do things by threat, all that stuff. So you can't accuse me of giving it out but not being able to take it.

(the words of someone who has been a bully)

My personal definition of bullying is to do with that nasty kind of mental or physical mistreatment that happens on a long-term basis. If it's a one-off thing I would not say it was bullying, more like a dispute. But if the same young person is being picked on all the time, you know the one who is always pushed to the back of the line, or their pens disappear, or they are kicked, punched, or suffer name calling, that definitely constitutes bullying for me.

Yes, and bullying can take on a racial dimension as well. Basically this happens where anyone is picked on because of their skin colour. Black and Asian youngsters face this in some places on a daily basis, both inside and outside school. Teachers have a major responsibility when it happens in school to deal with it – to challenge the behaviour of those who are involved.

It is this challenging of bullying behaviour, in whatever guise it takes, that is all-important. In my school we decided to take a positive stand against bullying that directly involved both young people and staff. Our response was geared directly towards prevention. We started what is called a peer mediation scheme, with the primary intention of letting young people themselves sort out their own disputes and problems. We found that staff spent a great deal of time dealing with 'low level' disputes. Yet, we also recognised that these can often spill over into something far more serious and potentially lead to full-blown bullying behaviour. The staff themselves recognised that there was a need to find a better way of dealing with these kinds of matters, and it was one of them who suggested the idea of pupil mediation.

On the surface the scheme itself sounds very simple to operate. In a sense we see mediation as pre-bullying, giving young people the skills to deal with disputes before they get out of hand. And yes, it has to fit into a wider strategy of providing information about bullying to young people and their parents, and of having the mechanisms in place to deal with serious incidents that require teacher and parental intervention. But crucially we gave the idea support and recognition from the start. We believed in the ability of pupils to resolve their own difficulties without always having to expect, or need, adult intervention.

The scheme is a self-help scheme, and therefore requires a group of young people to act in the role of mediators. The intention is to get all the parties involved in any incident together in a mediation session and give them the opportunity to tell their side of the story. Mediation is a voluntary activity, so there has to be a willingness to participate by everyone concerned. The mediators' role is to listen, assess what is happening, reflect their view of the events to those involved, check out the accuracy of that view, and explore the underlying causes of the behaviour. But more than that, it is to assist in creating some kind of resolution to the problem by asking those involved what they think is the way forward. That's the difficult bit, bearing in mind there are no adults available to offer 'friendly' guidance. This is why we have made a major investment in training the mediators to perform their role.

So how have we gone about training our mediators? Well, we started off by offering the opportunity to train as a mediator to the whole of a year group. We concentrated on things like the need to work together to find solutions to problems, to raise individual self-esteem through playing communication games, to actually encourage people to say positive things about each other and receive criticism. We talked about how you go about articulating your feelings. This was the preliminary stage, but it was vital in that we were able to explore the ideas behind mediation from very early on.

From there we took a chance. We asked the pupils to decide on who they thought would make the most effective mediators. This was done in a positive and not an excluding way. We stressed that everyone had the potential, but perhaps some people were better suited than others at the time. They had to think very carefully about the qualities and skills of the mediator. Now, it has to be said that some of the staff were nervous, and indeed, some wanted to pick the mediators for themselves. Yet funnily, it turned out that the young people selected almost the same group as would have been selected by the staff. What does that say about the judgement of young people?

From there the pupils who were voted to act as mediators received a further two days' training on actually practising mediation. In all we have a mediation team of some 15 young people. They operate the system for themselves. They are the ones who are largely approached when a mediation session is needed. They take control in the session and make sure things run according to the procedures that have been established.

The mediation scheme started in January 1994. From the beginning I realised that the training of the pupils would need a great deal of time, effort and resource allocation. It was going to involve a whole year group who have many other pressures placed on them. So I wanted to monitor what was going on. We established a disputes register in which all requests for mediation were logged. The outcomes of mediation sessions were carefully recorded and I spoke with pupils and staff on a regular basis to see how things were developing. In the first instance disputes rose. In part I think the young people were trying out the system. Perhaps they wanted to see how it worked, or if the adults would really leave them alone to sort out their problems. And yes, I'm happy to say that since the scheme was introduced disputes have dropped and the school does appear to be a happier place.

The other thing I want to say is that this approach, I am sure, could be used elsewhere. Bullying happens all over the place, in children's homes, youth clubs, etc. With mediation there is an opportunity to say in a very open way that interpersonal relationships are important and they can be improved if we try. The scheme also offers an avenue for the potential 'victim' and 'perpetrator' of bullying to come together and present their views of the world. We try and get to the problem early before it escalates. But vitally we convey the message that young people are capable and, with training and support, will solve many of their own problems.

Lucy Griffiths
Headteacher, The Jessons School, Dudley

21
Mental Health and Save
the Children's Rights Work

This chapter describes the work of Save the Children in its attempts to promote rights-based work around the issue of mental health.

A picture of mental health

This chapter suggests how a rights framework may help to provide a more positive and sensitive understanding of the mental health needs of disadvantaged young people and describes how Save the Children projects in the UK are helping to promote mental health using rights-based approaches. Examples are taken from projects working with young people, most of whom are in their teens and early twenties.

Some recent issues brought to Save the Children projects by young people have included low self-esteem, lack of assertiveness, effects of sexual abuse, drugs misuse, eating disorders, stress, domestic violence, burglary, effects of racial exclusion and racial assault. All have mental health connections.

Save the Children is an international charity committed to making a reality of the rights of children and young adults. Its projects (currently 80 in the United Kingdom) work with disadvantaged and marginalised children and young people, in the families and communities in which they live, on issues of significance to them. Young people and project workers are increasingly identifying and articulating concerns which they themselves relate to mental health.

It is not breaking new ground to suggest that any person's mental health should be seen as a positive attribute – as with other aspects of health. However, set against social and cultural norms and current trends towards ever more straitened health resource allocation, this ideal of mental health in the UK is far from being realised. The tarnished picture is partly about individual and community perceptions. In contrast to other aspects of health in society, mental illness is still, often, a labelling term – the butt of jokes, a cause of embarrassment and a taboo demanding isolation. It is equally about responses of policy makers and service providers. Community care (Department of Health, 1990) has done little to break down views of mental health as being mainly about illness and problems.

Mental health and young people

For young people the picture becomes still bleaker. Those under 18 years old have no vote and their opinions may be regarded less; many are outside the labour market (and are viewed as particularly exploitable consumers) with no income support until aged 18; and they have minimal control over sometimes hostile media portraits.

Thus, at the stages of personal development when questions about identity and needs for privacy, confidentiality and respect arise, the expression of such needs and susceptibility to external pressures are strong psychological influences. Young people may meet with adult responses that suppress, ignore and undervalue them. The total effect on a young person's confidence and well-being may be profound and, sometimes, shattering.

Young people who have sought help from services sometimes say, in retrospect, that their original hope was simply to find someone to listen. But many statutory services artificially divide activities into identifiable problems and between a host of professionals – social workers, psychologists, educational specialists, youth court officers, and so on. To expect young people to successfully engage with so many systems, themselves in flux, is to ask a great deal.

Recent reports (see Department of Health, 1995; NHS Health Advisory Service, 1995; Kurtz, 1994) have highlighted the absence of specific community mental health service provision for children and young people and have criticised the lack of local joint strategic planning between health and social services. Variability and patchiness are the main service characteristics. The strengthening of primary care provision and an integrated youth mental health service (offering assessment, care and intervention) are needed.

A further twist is that services may have particular difficulty in finding out about and meeting the needs of young people where these are greatest. Less accessible, less motivated young people who, for example, experience school exclusion, emotional, drug, or alcohol problems, trouble with the police or homelessness, may be labelled by these services as just disruptive (British Association of Community Child Health, 1995).

Save the Children's perspective and young people's rights

Save the Children's overall approach is to start working with young people on what they themselves want, building on their strengths. This means that we are usually asking people to make an active contribution so that they feel valued and respected in a way that they would not if they were passive recipients of services.

We also encourage young people to think about personal problems in a broader context, which may help in itself (for example, it's not your fault if you are homeless) and to be of practical assistance in addressing the problems in question. It is also an approach which links directly to a rights-based understanding of children's and young people's abilities, needs and status.

The UN Convention on the Rights of the Child, ratified by the UK in 1991, covers the rights of every person under 18 years. It addresses a gamut of concerns, including those in relation to young people's mental health. Underpinning rights (relating to protection, provision and participation) are concerned with non-discrimination (Article 2: all rights apply equally to all young people); the child's best interests (Article 3: decisions affecting a young person must fully consider what is best for them); and their opinions (Article 12: a young person has a right to opinions which must be listened to).

Of particular importance to young people and their mental health are rights to the best chance to fully develop, to information and expression, to freedom of thought, to meet with others, to privacy, to the best possible health and care, to education, to participation, and to protection from exploitation. The denial of a basic right like education (for example, through school exclusion) can itself trigger mental health problems.

Project practice within Save the Children

Projects highlight the connections between rights and mental health by encouraging young people to meet together and participate. A common theme in direct work with young people is the importance of developing trust. Such rights as freedom of expression and from exploitation can be undermined without it:

> I felt I wasn't accepted or understood . . . just a stupid girl who'd got pregnant young. In fact I was a mother, wanting to make friends. (young single mother: Whalen, 1993)

The fact that trust is identified as an essential building block suggests how young people's mental health and other needs are bound together. Trust appears to be a good indicator of how successful participants will be in gaining each other's respect, sharing confidence or raising self-esteem. To obtain young people's trust within community settings depends on two underlying factors. Projects must have good local reputations, must be well established and not stigmatising, in the opinion of potential clients. They must also work at the client's pace on the issues that matter to him or her. For projects to fulfil either obligation a key resource is time.

Personal issues and development

Contact by young people with all projects is voluntary. They often first drop in 'for a cup of coffee and a chat'. They may visit only once or regularly over several years. Projects offer a range of services (for example, from laundry facilities to confidential counselling). Thus, there is a choice of entry points and, more importantly, young people see that their integrity is respected. They are not treated as 'special cases' (that is, unusually disadvantaged or disruptive).

What happens when a young person seems worried, depressed, or confused, and requests help? Of prime importance is that project workers are prepared to listen:

> They won't tell you what to do . . . they'll listen to what you've got to say . . . and work with you on what you want to achieve. (leaflet, The Warren, Hull, 1996)

Project workers recognise young people's rights to exercise judgement and control over their own situations. Outsiders should not be saying unilaterally how, or with whom, these are to be addressed. Again, time is vital to listen well, to assist young people to understand past experiences that may have profoundly demotivated them in their capacity for independence and self-assertion. Some young people have spent long periods in institutions with no real right of privacy:

> If you are in care you have privacy from the other young people but not from the adults . . . the staff can come in whenever they want. (Rights for Us Group, 1994)

An absence of privacy reduces young people's control over their situations and, in turn, may limit their opportunities to express concerns. That their rights are so interconnected equates with the views of young people described already: that their mental health needs are indivisible too. Only when confronted with the piece-meal provision of most statutory services do they find that these needs cannot easily be accommodated.

Working in community settings means that projects need to offer support in different directions and at different levels. With project workers' support, the young person may need to prioritise problems in order to cope with underlying mental health concerns. Someone who is homeless and hungry needs accommodation, food and financial help before they can deal with emotional problems or their alcoholism.

At BYPASS, a young people's project in Bolton, young people are free to go to external counsellors but often prefer to use those in the project. They want a safe environment where they already feel comfortable and secure:

> When I came to BYPASS I was a real mess. I didn't have any confidence . . . I had counselling in hospital but it never worked for me. But here the counsellor asks me how I feel about things. (Shanks, 1995)

Involvement with services and group activity

BYPASS networks with local community psychiatric nurses (CPNs) who already support individual young people at the project. The open nature of these meetings – to discuss issues, not individuals – has resulted in better relations between the project and CPNs and specific improvements on key issues for young people, such as medication and appointment systems.

Through links with statutory agencies, projects promote mental health further afield. Strabane Family Centre, Northern Ireland, successfully developed yoga-based relaxation techniques with the local youth services after young people at youth centres identified themselves as being under stress at school, in families and from peer pressure. The young people had described some of their former responses to stress as getting drunk, self-mutilation and feeling suicidal.

Their community locations mean that projects naturally tend towards group work as young people's personal issues develop and clarify themselves. The Niddrie project, in Edinburgh, worked with ten 14–15 year old women, almost half of whom were bulimic. These young women found mutual support from the others whilst the whole group benefited by discussing how these and parallel concerns were dealt with at school and amongst families.

Group discussion allows young people to concentrate on what links their situations, rather than their isolation. This may lead them to use existing services. The young women with bulimia accepted referral to a specialist hospital department. They found the experience positive and Niddrie staff took no further direct action. Instead, they have developed related work on self-support and mutual understanding for young women's groups, with a Brook Advisory Centre.

At Lifechance, in Oxford, much developmental work takes place in groups. The rationale is in a critique of approaches which become too focused on the individual. Many young people who visit Lifechance have been in care. Local authorities do not always accommodate young people over 16 years old and care leavers may become homeless, unemployed and lack basic support. Being forced into such situations can inflict mental harm.

Groups are encouraged to campaign on issues they raise, advocating on their own behalf with local authorities and others. Their common concerns are likely to be those of other young people in similar situations. Group members gain the confidence to do something about their own needs, as well as seeing how their actions benefit their peers.

In joint meetings with health authorities and services, young people at Lifechance explored pertinent issues such as accessibility, drugs advice and sexual health. They are now conducting health authority funded research to find out about peer views on health issues, with a focus on mental health.

This peer research method has already been tested nationally by young care leavers involved with Save the Children projects, to determine the general concerns of other young care leavers (West, 1995). Mental health was an important concern, closely allied to the support needs that these young people had:

> Support is someone to be there to help you and back you up. Also young people have the 'right to fail' now and again.

Young people at risk

The Warren, in Hull, is a multi-purpose, voluntary resource centre in which Save the Children workers participate. It runs a weekly group for 11–16 year olds who are 'at risk'. Many are excluded from school, have been in local authority care, have run away from parental or children's homes, or are in trouble with the police. Most have spent some time living on the street. A risk assessment procedure (RAP) has been written specifically for this group, all of whose members know about it and why it is necessary.

When police, social services or other authorities make contact with the group, or a worker is concerned about the risk a young person faces, the young person and worker discuss what the young person wants to do and what the worker's responsibilities under the RAP are. One option is for the young person to leave the centre, as workers cannot hold young people against their will.

The right to leave is respected by statutory agencies, although this may mean that the young person is placing him/herself in a vulnerable situation. In practice, the open discussion with the young person means that this option of last resort is infrequently taken. Spending time to talk about choices and preferred outcomes is time well spent, for the young person usually feels more in control as a result, and the action agreed has a far better chance of success.

Looking ahead

Save the Children is working with young people who have thought hard about mental health issues. In a face-to-face questionnaire, young people (aged from 14 to 20 years) at the Kensington and Chelsea Leaving Care Project said that mental health should not only have negative connotations:

> Mental health is the state your mind is in – whether you're in good . . . or bad mental health. (young man, aged 17)

The examples, from various Save the Children projects, have shown that to have the opportunity to explore mental health, in personal and wider terms, is not likely to be a source of trouble or confusion to vulnerable young people. Rather, the reverse is true: their difficulties multiply where they have no voice.

These examples demonstrate, too, how young people are successfully engaged already in positive dialogue and action to improve their mental health opportunities. Under the UN Convention on the Rights of the Child, young people in the UK now have recognised rights to be heard and to be involved in how the agenda develops. Health and other agencies need to recognise this and take appropriate action to ensure that many more young people are able to exercise their rights.

Notes

Many thanks to Kieran Breen, Marilyn Davies, Hilary Groom, Sophie Laws, Bridget Pettitt, Mary Roddy and Anna Whalen, all of Save the Children, for their advice and information.

References

British Association of Community Child Health (1995) *Child Health Rights: Implementing the UN Convention on the Rights of the Child within the National Health Service*, London: BACCH.

Department of Health (1995) *A Handbook on Child and Adolescent Mental Health*, London: DoH.

Department of Health (1990) *NHS and Community Care Act*, London: HMSO.

Kurtz, Z. (1994) *Services for the Mental Health of Children and Young People in England: a National Review*, London: South Thames Regional Health Authority.

NHS Health Advisory Service (1995) *Together We Stand: the Commissioning, Role and Management of Child and Adolescent Mental Health Services*, London: HMSO.

Rights for Us Group (1994) *A Guide to Rights: by Young People for Young People, from the UN Convention*, London: Save the Children.

Shanks, K. (1995) *BYPASS: the Awareness of Health*, Dublin: Virtual Image.

West, A. (1995) *You're On Your Own: Young People's Research on Leaving Care*, London: Save the Children.

Whalen, A. (1993) *Try On My Shoes: Youth Work with Young Women in the 1990s*, London: Save the Children.

Christopher Cuninghame
Save the Children

22

A Friend in Need

Here West Midlands Lesbian and Gay Switchboard talk about how they can help and support young people who want to 'come out'.

What West Midlands Lesbian and Gay Switchboard offers is anonymous advice and information. We are another gay voice. A voice that people can actually speak to, but will never meet.

We ask people to have been 'out' for two years before they operate a switchboard because we believe you need to have had the experience your clients will be ringing you about. We want you to have gone through some of the trials and tribulations of coming out, and the joys of making lesbian and gay friends, and having heterosexual friends who accept your sexuality. The whole experience of working at Switchboard is based on your life experience.

Lesbian and gay youth groups

There's two lesbian and gay youth groups in Birmingham. The one that meets on a Saturday has some funding from the city council, but they're having some hassle. The centre they meet at doesn't want them there: they want these queers out!

The projects tend to get used by, say, young people who live in Birmingham. There's also a youth group in Coventry, but in Wolverhampton, Walsall, Sandwell, Shropshire, Staffordshire . . . there's nothing. It's an identified need. There are lots of young lesbians and gays out there who, because there isn't a youth group for them to go to, end up coming on to the commercial lesbian and gay scene and going to bars at quite a young age. So it can be like forcing a lot of young lesbians and gays to grow up a lot quicker than they're ready to.

Age of consent?

When we're talking to someone under the age of 18, we point out what the law is, so they're aware of the age of consent. We don't hide behind the law, but this covers us legally.

We will not encourage or discourage any sexual activity. We *will* try and ensure they're practising safer sex, and if they're very active, we might talk to them about having a hepatitis B jab.

There's still a lot of confusion about the age of consent, because a lot of people didn't actually realise when it became law. We still get phone calls checking what the age of consent is, not just from young people but from older people who may be attracted to someone and they're not sure what their legal status is. The way I understand the law is that it still refers to consent as being related to anal intercourse. So they're very confused as to whether a young man can consent to oral sex, or any other sexual activity. Now, under law he *can't*, but the law is very confusing as to what you're actually prosecuted for. The law is not about your ability to consent to sexual *activity*. It's about your ability to consent to sexual *acts*, and the law makers are not sure or not willing to admit that certain sexual acts are common sexual activities.

If under 18, a gay man is considered not capable of being gay, but he's capable of dying for his country. We have to tell young people that, so that they know there is a risk. That often depends on who gets involved if under-age sexual activity is discovered. As I understand it, under the Children Act, after their 17th birthday, social services aren't going to give a shit. The police normally won't get involved either. However, if one of them's 16 and one of them's 30, then it's far more likely that the police'll get involved, than if one of them's 17 and the other's 19. There's no consideration given to the fact that the 16/30 relationship could be far more loving and less manipulative than the 17/19 one.

Censorship and promotion

There's never been a prosecution under Section 28 and it's unlikely that there ever will be, partly because under a later Education Act they removed sex education from local authority control anyway and took it down to school governor level. So there's a lot of confusion as to what that section of the Act was supposed to do. We *can* go into schools and youth groups and we *have* been into schools and youth groups. Last year, for instance we went and spoke to a Venture Scouts group, 'cos one of them had come out to the rest of his group and he invited us to go in and talk to them. He felt he wanted some support, and that's how he wanted it done, and apparently it was one of the best nights they'd had. We even did training on preventing teenage pregnancies – part of our argument being that if you make young lesbians and gays comfortable they won't get themselves pregnant, or get someone else pregnant, in order to prove how 'straight' they are.

Coming out

You have to be aware of the risks of coming out. If you scream it at the top of your voice when you're 15 in school, you're more than likely going to get beaten up. If you tell your local youth group that you're gay, not only may the workers not be able to cope with it, they may not be able to cope with other kids threatening you. The support systems for young lesbians and gays aren't there. Not in the statutory sector anyway. They just don't recognise it as a need that should be funded properly.

More often than not, young lesbians and gays will tell you that they were scared to ring you. They will break down in tears while they are talking to you. Or they will tell you about themselves being beaten up. Or they will tell you that they tried suicide. You're scared to talk to your friends, your *best* friends who you've always shared everything with. You're scared to tell your parents, you're scared to tell anyone. And with HIV and AIDS happening, it's become a bigger taboo for gay men. I'm from the generation that has been going to funerals regularly for 10 years. If you're actually experiencing death as part of your growing-up process, then that's scary as well. You hear young gay men coming out with crap like, 'it's an older gay male disease', but unfortunately on some things unless you listen, not to your elders and betters, but the ones who learnt hardest, *you are going to die*. And there's nowt worse than counselling someone who's 16 and positive.

Now, I don't want this to get morbid. We have actually learnt to love each other and love ourselves, and take joy from the lives of those we have lost. Young people have to experience that as well.

Finding a friend

We encourage young lesbians and gays to join a peer group they feel comfortable in. That's another service that the Birmingham gay youth group provides. It's a stepping stone so that they can then go out on the commercial gay scene, or elsewhere, and they've got some lesbian and gay friends. So you're not walking into a nightclub, which can hold 1,300 people, by yourself, and there's also someone looking out for you. That makes the gay scene sound very predatory, which it can be, but there's a whole community feel there.

If people are lonely, or shy, or scared of going onto the commercial gay scene, then we will, at Switchboard, offer a thing called 'a befriending' where two operators (and if the client is under 18 we say these have to be a man and a woman) go out and meet someone and take them wherever that person wants to go, on a totally non-sexual basis. A lot of lesbians and gay men on the commercial scene will provide this alternative support group or alternative family for a lot of young people. We remember what it was like and we have some general responsibilities. It's also about watching their backs and telling the little sods to shut up when they're being noisy! In the gay community you can be forced to grow up very quickly and most of them grow up as well adjusted as any other adult.

Andy Chaffer
West Midlands Lesbian and Gay Switchboard

Interview by Daren Garratt
The Open University

23

Acting as an Appropriate Adult

This chapter focuses on the specific role of the social worker who acts as an 'appropriate adult' when young people are in custody.

The introduction of the Police and Criminal Evidence Act (PACE) in 1984 brought with it, for those who are detained and considered 'vulnerable' under the Act, the safeguard of the presence of an appropriate adult during their interview.

> It is important to bear in mind that, although juveniles or persons who are mentally disordered or handicapped are often capable of providing reliable evidence, they may, without knowing or wishing to do so, be particularly prone in certain circumstances to providing information which is unreliable, misleading or self-incriminating. (PACE Codes of Practice 1991, Notes for Guidance 11B)

The Codes of Practice under that Act (Home Office, 1991) provide both a definition of a vulnerable suspect and the duties and responsibilities of the appropriate adult.

The absence of an appropriate adult will not necessarily invalidate any evidence obtained from the vulnerable suspect. If there is a delay in an appropriate person arriving at the police station and an officer of the rank of superintendent or above considers that to delay interview would involve an immediate risk of harm to persons or serious damage to property, then he may sanction the interview.

Social workers should take particular note if they find that on arrival at the police station such an interview has already taken place. A note of it should have been made on the custody record and the detainee's solicitor may also find it important at a later stage.

Once the custody officer has decided on the need for an appropriate adult, that person should be sent for. The primary function of the role is to be an adult who will provide comfort and support to a child who might otherwise be disorientated in such strange surroundings. This adult is intended to be someone who will take an interest in the well-being of the child, and know them sufficiently well to recognise signs of distress. The adult should always check that if the child has been detained over the period of a mealtime, they have been offered food and drink. The detained person should have had sufficient sleep and be alert enough to answer questions. They should not be under the influence of alcohol or drugs, or be placed under any undue pressure. While the parent or guardian of a juvenile would obviously be the best person to assess the child's physical and mental well-being, they may not necessarily have the experience or confidence needed to represent the child effectively in the potentially hostile atmosphere of the custody suite.

If the juvenile in question is in the care of, or accommodated by, the local authority, then a carer from the home or voluntary organisation would be thought the best person to stand in for the parent. Although a juvenile's primary carer may be considered the ideal person there are also incidents when this person would be the most inappropriate adult to act on the child's behalf. The Codes of Practice C, Notes for Guidance 1C, tells us that:

> The parent or guardian of a juvenile should be the appropriate adult unless he is suspected of involvement in the offence, is the victim, is involved in the investigation, or has received admissions. In such circumstances it would be desirable for the appropriate adult to be some other person. If the parent of a juvenile is estranged from the juvenile, he should not be asked to act as the appropriate adult if the juvenile expressly objects to his presence.

As far as social workers are concerned a situation containing a 'conflict of interest' is most likely to arise for the residential social worker. When acting as the court liaison officer for my employing authority I was on one occasion asked, by a defence solicitor in court, why the local authority had allowed a residential worker, who had been on duty at the time that the offence was discovered in the home, to act as an appropriate adult. As staff from the residential unit were the only witnesses to the boy's crime, the defence maintained (and rightly so) that they could not then act impartially in his best interests. In cases where a residential worker may have been physically assaulted by a young person in their care, a social worker from another authority should act as appropriate adult. Workers from the same authority may be considered colleagues and have a loyalty towards each other, which would make it difficult for them to act in a completely impartial way.

The Codes of Practice make a clear point that a solicitor acting in his/her professional capacity cannot also act as an appropriate adult. The solicitor is there solely to protect the client's interests, whereas the appropriate adult has a broader role:

to advise the person being questioned and to observe whether or not the interview is being conducted properly and fairly and to facilitate communication between the person being questioned and the police.

Social workers need to be careful in explaining what their role is to the young person being questioned, and how they do this, particularly in relation to admissions of guilt.

If the young person has not requested a solicitor, then the social worker's role is to advise them of the advantages of doing so. In my experience, as an appropriate adult, this can often prove a 'sticking point' with both the young person and the police. Often the juveniles that a social worker is called to are those who are frequent visitors to the custody suite. This might be the reason their parents refuse to attend. These young people may like to think of themselves as 'old hands' knowing as much as any solicitor. They certainly know that if a solicitor is called, it will increase their time in the cell. Police too, who are anxious to process the juveniles swiftly, will often bring pressure to bear at this point. They may say to the detainee in front of the social worker, 'You don't want a solicitor, you just want to get out of here, don't you?', thus implying that they are the child's true 'friend', not the social worker. At this point the appropriate adult may override the wishes of the juvenile and insist on a solicitor being present. This may be thought necessary to protect the rights of the detainee who may not understand the significance of what is being said to him. Having done this, against the stated wishes of the juvenile, it will then take all the worker's skill to re-establish a rapport with the young person. I have felt the wrath of the custody officer; on one occasion I was made to stand and wait for the solicitor's arrival, which took three hours (there was no chair available in the whole of the station!). On another occasion I was made to wait in my car (at night), this time there being no room in the entire police station for me! Other colleagues have similar stories. This attitude is by no means uniform throughout the force, but where it does arise I feel the reasons may be twofold. Firstly, the police always seem to think that the presence of a solicitor will mean a 'no comment interview'. Secondly, the importance of police culture cannot be understated. The police may on occasions feel they 'know' who has committed a particular offence, and they do not want the interference of solicitors and 'do-gooding' social workers to allow the guilty to walk free.

Evans (1993), commenting on research by Evans and Ferguson (1991), states that all three categories, parents, solicitors and social workers, are notoriously slow to intervene during the interview process. When parents intervene it can often be to the detriment of their children. They put pressure on them to own up, often loudly declaring that they are old enough to know better or that they will wash their hands of them. Perhaps these parents feel embarrassed or stigmatised by their children's wrongdoing and wish to be seen to disassociate themselves.

Evans concludes (1993: 40):

> although parents are generally passive observers of their children's interviews they contribute substantially more than professionals. Solicitors attended interviews in approximately 11 per cent (18) of cases; in 9 of these the police used persuasive tactics and obtained a confession. Social workers, who were mainly residential workers responsible for the care of the children being interviewed or specialist juvenile justice workers, attended interviews in approximately 19 per cent (29) of cases. In 18 of these cases the police used persuasive tactics and obtained a confession. (Evans, 1993)

Finally, how does the appropriate adult know when they should intervene in a police interview? The Codes of Practice give us our guidelines: 'No officer may try to obtain answers to questions or elicit a statement by use of oppression, or shall indicate, except in answer to a direct question, what action will be taken on the part of the police if the person being interviewed answers questions, makes a statement or refuses to do either' (Codes of Practice, C, 11.3).

At the beginning of the interview, along with the normal introductions, the appropriate adult should be made fully aware of their role. My personal experience is that the interviewing officer will tell the social worker or parent that they are there not merely as an observer but to befriend and assist the interviewee, and have the right to stop the interview at any time.

When first addressing the suspect, the police officer should state clearly in connection with what offence the juvenile is to be questioned. It is often a tactic used by police at this stage to let the young person guess what they are to be questioned about. This can be in the form of a leading question: 'you do know why you're here, don't you?' Even when the person doesn't know why they are there, they are invited to say they do. The police hope, of course, that they will keep talking and unwittingly make a confession. In the Evans and Ferguson (1991) research it was revealed that the researchers had difficulty in identifying the exact legal offence for which some of the juveniles in their sample were being dealt with. Out of 164 taped interviews, 38.5% of suspects were not told precisely what offence they were being questioned about.

References

Evans, R. (1993) *The Royal Commission on Criminal Justice. The Conduct of Police Interviews with Juveniles*, Research Study no. 8. London: HMSO.

Evans, R. and Ferguson, T. (1991) 'Comparing different juvenile cautionary systems in one police area'. Report to the Home Office Research and Planning Unit.

Home Office (1991) *The Police and Criminal Evidence Act 1984: Codes of Practice*, London: Home Office.

Marie Kearns
Youth Justice Worker

24

Someone Who Really Cares

How important are supportive and caring relationships to young people as they grow up? Here we look at some of the ideas and theories that have informed work in this area.

> It's brilliant here . . . they love me and include me in the family . . . I hope I will stay here until I am 18. (Angela, aged 14)
>
> Cliffe and Berridge, *Closing Children's Homes*

> My closest friend during those days was a young nun, a novice of barely nineteen or twenty . . . Her friendship towards me and the love I felt towards her were in marked contrast to my feelings for the nuns in the School of Cappoquin, who were by now nothing more to me than bad memories.
>
> Paddy Doyle, *The God Squad*

> Miss Temple . . . her friendship and society had been my continual solace; she had stood me in the stead of a mother, governess, and, latterly companion.
>
> Charlotte Brontë, *Jane Eyre*

Each of the above quotations illustrates how important just one supportive relationship can be to a young person facing difficulties. In the first instance, Angela has had a series of foster placements and, whilst the author describes her as still feeling unsettled and demonstrating behaviours which her foster parents find unacceptable, she feels cared for and secure. Indeed she says her foster parents love her. In the second quote, Paddy Doyle is describing his experience of hospitalisation after neglectful care in the industrial school system in Ireland. The nun's friendship is of massive importance to him. It is therapeutic in easing some of Paddy's painfully bad memories and in helping him to endure harsh hospital conditions. In the final quote, the fictitious character Jane Eyre explains how life in boarding school is made bearable because of the presence of just one kind individual. It is clear that one adult who is capable of making a young person feel cared about can be crucial in enabling that individual to cope with and overcome difficulties.

It is important to remember that adults can and do make a difference. A relationship with someone who really cares may be the only thing keeping a young person from feeling total despair, giving up, offending, etc. However, when much media coverage is given to abusive relationships between adults and young people, it is possible to lose sight of the fact that the vast majority of adults are not dangerous. Many may genuinely want to help the young people with whom they come into contact.

Whilst friends, relatives, befrienders and mentors are of key importance in supporting and motivating young people who face difficulties, the major focus here will be on adults providing care in the residential settings of foster homes, children's homes and special residential schools. This area is worthy of particular attention because of the significant issues and dilemmas presented by residential care. Also a recent study of children in care in the 1990s noted that the young people in residential care today present a greater concentration of difficulties than their predecessors. The problems currently perceived are claimed to arise from young people entering the care system as a result of a final breakdown in family relationships, or from adolescents already in care experiencing a crisis of disordered or challenging behaviour.

The discussion that follows is used to highlight some understandings of what is considered important for successful caring, using a range of perspectives from across a large time span. The amount of agreement on the qualities required of a successful carer is remarkable.

The natural

The qualities required of carers are those of commitment to children and a personality that might be summed up as 'the salt of the earth'. The latter suggests someone whose goodwill knows no bounds and who is capable of gaining others' trust. As far back as the nineteenth century, Thomas Bowman Stephenson wanted his care workers to be seen as heads of a family, and he instructed them to endeavour to act in a way that led individuals to treat them with the respect, confidence and affection which children should feel for their parents. He was convinced that love would be a carer's greatest strength (Wilson, 1966). Similarly, Dr Barnardo, perhaps the most famous provider of child care in history, looked for 'good material' in his staff appointments. What 'good material' meant was that applicants who claimed a fondness for children would be highly regarded, and Barnardo thought this was of greater relevance than knowledge or experience of child care

(Williams, 1943). In 1946 England's first child care officers were established to fulfil important roles in a major social services initiative. Again, child care officers' qualities were emphasised as being on the personal side (despite the fact that they were also expected to be graduates). They were to be genial and friendly, able to set both children and adults at their ease.

In 1988, Kahan interviewed recipients of care about their experiences. Their views echo those presented above. She explains that at the time when most of those people she interviewed were in care, official attitudes to training and child care policy generally were discouraging residential child care workers from attempting to be substitute parents and encouraging what was believed to be a more professional approach to the task. However her interviewees were unaware of this trend and were thus uninhibited by it in the emphasis which they gave to their own priorities! They needed residential workers to play a substitute parenting role, whether staff wished to or not. These ex-residents explained themselves very clearly. They wanted 'mum' substitutes. They appreciated workers who listened, and had a soft spot for children. The ex-residents believed workers should be married, with experience of parenting and loving, and were very critical of one group home where the staff were liberal in attitude and acted more like contemporaries than parents. It seems that these ex-residents wanted the security, boundaries and care of 'traditional' parenting (Kahan, 1988).

The following description is of Meg Plover, a foster carer, who was particularly successful in her care of a large foster family. The writer was a field worker who was also involved with the family. The passage is used here because of the richness of the image portrayed. Meg is hugely successful, full of good common-sense qualities, and has the capacity to be able to make day-to-day living therapeutic, thus healing and helping those in her care to overcome their difficulties and difficult circumstances. The field worker who praises Meg understands that it is her intelligence, and her insight into the children's behaviour, that result in success.

> Meg Plover tried to provide the security and consistent affection which they [the young people] lacked. She is depicted as a warm, caring, ebullient woman, strongly partial to the children who claimed her as 'Auntie'. She worked hard to create an affectionate unit and achieved something close to a family base for a small group of children. She had little or no illusions that she could fully compensate the children for the loss of their own parents or that it was possible in residential care to provide a real sense of family. She established a caring base for them, which they called 'home' and to which they continued to look for

support long after they had grown up. Meg Plover had a great gift of fun and laughter and was able to make ordinary routine events enjoyable as well as showing her exasperation at times. (Mann, 1984)

Maier (1985) believes that this type of care has to be underpinned by insight into child development and knowledge of human behaviour. He describes the following scene in a residential home to illustrate how day-to-day living can be made therapeutic by a care worker. The suggestion here is that these workers have insight into why their particular care is helping to make a difference.

> 'Try these soft pillows' says a group care worker who is handing cushions to a number of fifteen year old girls sprawled out across the floor for an evening of television watching. 'I turned up the heat in the bathroom, so it will be good and warm when you get out of the shower', remarked another care worker. Concerns for bodily comfort, like straightening out children's blankets at bedtime in order to make them more comfortable for the night, or sitting down with a child on the floor so that the youngster can afford a more relaxed body posture and eye contact, are common child care activities. But however spontaneous or mundane, this quality of caring is vital and should not be overlooked. Throughout life a sense of well-being and caring is closely related to the degree of bodily security and comfort a person experiences. (Maier, 1985)

In reality most residential carers have few opportunities to see their work from any kind of theoretical perspective. Chances to examine their practice and value the care task, in any kind of planned or systematic way, are minimal. The majority of staff employed in residential care in Britain lack a relevant qualification. Residential care is still dominated by historical attitudes towards looking after children, seeing residential care as women's work, in which the skills are inherent or intuitive and the commitment of the workforce is exploitable. While the skills and difficulties associated with the care context are exceptional, more training is needed at all levels. It seems crucial that residential care workers should know and understand the premises upon which their work is based. It is this knowledge that allows understanding of why what appear to be natural qualities (embodying good-heartedness and a love of children) are so highly valued and count for so much.

Theoretical underpinning

Theoretical understandings which underpin the demand for this therapeutic kind of residential practice (and therefore the qualities required of care workers) are based on the understanding that early, previous or existing relationships in these young persons' lives have caused damage and hurt which prevent or impede their ability to form successful relationships. Having belief in one's own worth has been shown to be crucial to successful development (Coopersmith, 1967). MacNamara explains the situation well when she writes about dealing with children with emotional and behavioural difficulties in school:

> One common reaction from pupils who are damaged is that they feel so badly already that they cannot tolerate anything else that increases that bad feeling and so they put up defences in order to not hear anything. In this way they reduce the chances of being hurt anymore . . . What these pupils are in effect saying is that they will not allow anyone to reach them, to touch them emotionally, and they will not allow themselves to have caring feelings for others in case they get hurt in the way they have been before. (1995: 15–16)

There is no doubt that childhood experiences can influence many factors in adulthood, particularly the pattern and stability of relationships (Rutter, 1981; 1985; Rutter and Quinton, 1984). There is no doubt either that much of the work of experts in the field of child care can be seen to be predicated on the belief that an especially strong emotional experience within a single relationship can be beneficial. Rothenburg (1977) worked with children and young people traumatised by their experiences of war and totally believed in the healing power of the depth and trust of her relationship with them. Barbara Dockar-Drysdale (1973) writes powerfully of the need for residential workers to become totally responsive to residents in an attempt to ensure that the young person is able to demand and receive the care he or she needs. Dockar-Drysdale describes life-changing and life-enhancing experiences for children when workers are prepared to respond by providing a type of care which would normally be associated with much younger children. More recently Adcock et al. (1989) have asserted that an especially strong emotional experience within a single relationship can break the pattern of earlier experiences. It is the skills exhibited in the giving of day-to-day residential care that make it possible to provide these emotionally corrective experiences.

Issues and dilemmas

David Wills, the head of a therapeutic community home for many years, wrote this description of the type of care he valued in his home.

Disturbed adolescents have frequently suffered grave impairment of the mother–child relationship, and the role of the woman worker is to be the target of feelings displaced from the mother to her, to understand them, and by skilled and patient understanding to help the boys work through them. Some boys have been denied much or all of that primary mother–child experience without which we cannot go forward to become separate 'other regarding' individuals. In such cases the woman worker has to try to provide primary experiences. All this is not only highly skilled work, it is work which puts them at the receiving end of much displaced animosity and hatred, which they have to accept and help the child, again, to work through if he is to make progress. In many such cases it is this primitive dependent relationship with a woman which enables a boy later to accept what is being offered by other people or other experiences. (1971: 121–3)

This is a particularly extreme position which many would see as outdated and indefensible in these days of feminism and workers' rights. However, it is included here because it demonstrates a particular care dilemma which is that certain tasks like the giving of physical and emotional comfort are established and remain women's work.

What follows is an extract from an interview with Karen, a 19 year old residential carer who 'really cares'. She begins by explaining how she sees her role.

My role is to be a professional member of care staff as much as possible and to learn to build a relationship with boys and learn to work. It is hard because the boys are going through puberty and things. They want to explore and find out and they do turn to me more at times because I'm their age.

Later she describes a professional dilemma that she faced as she tried to establish a relationship with Jake.

I was watching TV with Jake the other day and he had his arm around me. He had it tucked under my bottom and I didn't think anything of it. I just felt I was sitting on his hand but it was the fact that his finger would keep moving and I was thinking what does that mean. Is this meant to be dodgy or not? So I had to sort of tell him to move his hand up a bit and to say I want to be more comfortable and just little things like that. It's a case of whether it's on purpose or accidental. It's actually knowing what they're feeling . . . what they're thinking like.

Karen claims to be uncertain of whether this 15 year old, physically mature boy intends to wiggle his finger under her bottom. By staying confused about Jake's intentions Karen can avoid confrontation with him and to all intents and purposes their 'good relationship' will remain intact. This is important if Karen is to see herself as a successful professional. More insight into her dilemma was gleaned later in the same interview.

Interviewer: Have you ever had any problems with a boy because of closeness to them?

Karen: Anthony, I got on too friendly with him. It started getting . . . that's where I came close to almost . . . I think he might have started to build a relationship with boyfriend girlfriend terms so I had to sort of, like try to keep well away from him and he was . . . he'd try and push me to the limit and take me over the limit in how far our friendship could go?

Interviewer: Like what, can you give me an example?

Karen: Like he wanted to come round my house or he'd ask for cigarettes off me and try just be too friendly on a non-professional basis. Because I mean you have to always make sure you're being professional about it all.

Interviewer: How did that make you feel?

Karen: Very wary of what people thought of what's actually going on between us and um, very wary of how I felt about it all . . .

Interviewer: You were wondering if maybe they thought you were flirting with him?

Karen: Yes, sometimes, yes and also whether I was actually letting them see everything whereas I mean as far as they know I could have been doing like, letting him get up to all sorts of trouble when they were not about. Just letting him run riot.

Interviewer: When you say he pushed you to the limit can you give me an example of that?

Karen: Like umm he just punched me in a friendly way but too hard or umm he'd grope me. That was another thing he'd got into the habit of trying to do, trying to grope me which I didn't like.

Interviewer: What do you mean? Like putting his hand on your breast?

Karen: And other places. I've had to get quite nasty about it. I mean another incident where he came up friendly, kicked my legs away and I fell down and hurt myself, so I had to . . . He thought it was just a joke and I had to explain to him that it wasn't. I wasn't very good at explaining to him without swearing.

Sexual and physical harassment are a regular feature of Karen's working life. Yet because she feels that she is judged by her ability to form successful relationships with the boys she allows herself very little right of redress. It is shocking to see how she minimises the boys' behaviour but it is also understandable; she believes that if the boys misbehave she has failed. She fears that other workers will wrongly interpret her behaviour and see her as incompetent or colluding. Karen is a carer with great potential, and in possession of those natural qualities so demanded of carers, but she is being let down by a system which denies the complexity and difficulty of her work.

There is a general neglect of particular issues which may be associated with females giving care and handling the acting-out behaviours and sexuality of adolescents. This can be explained in part as due to the fact that only fairly recently has the residential child care population become so predominantly teenager focused. An additional problem is that generally it is assumed that residential workers, as agents of social control, are always the more powerful in resident/worker relations (Dominelli and McLeod, 1989) and any concern tends to centre on the abuse of power by adults (Stainton Rogers and Stainton Rogers, 1992). This professional discourse mutes any analysis about the general unacceptability of a range of adolescent male behaviour in the care context.

References

Adcock, M., Lake, R. and Small, A. (1989) 'Assessing children's need', in S. Morgan and P. Righton, *Child Care: Concerns and Conflicts*, London: Hodder and Stoughton.

Brontë, C. (1991) *Jane Eyre* (1847), London: Folio Society.

Cliffe, C. and Berridge, D. (1991) *Closing Children's Homes: an end to residential childcare?* London: National Children's Bureau.

Coopersmith, S. (1967) *The Antecedents of Self-Esteem*, San Francisco: W.H. Freeman.

Dominelli, L. and McLeod, E. (1989) *Feminist Social Work*, London: Macmillan.

Dockar-Drysdale, B. (1973) *Consultation in Child Care*, London: Longmans.

Doyle, P. (1988) *The God Squad*, Dublin: Raven Arts Press.

Kahan, B. (1988) *Growing Up in Care*, London: Basil Blackwell.

MacNamara, S. and Moreton, G. (1995) *Changing Behaviour: teaching children with emotional and behavioural difficulties in primary and secondary classrooms*, London: David Fulton.

Maier, H.W. (1985) 'Primary Care in secondary settings: inherent strains', in F. Ainsworth and L. Fulcher (eds), *Group Care Practice with Children*, London: Tavistock.

Mann, P. (1984) *Children in Care Revisited*. London: Batsford.

Rothenburg, M. (1977) *Children with Emerald Eyes*, London: Souvenir Press.

Rutter, M. (1981) *Maternal Deprivation Reassessed*, Harmondsworth: Penguin.

Rutter, M. (1985) 'Resilience in the face of adversity', *British Journal of Psychiatry*, 147: 598–611.

Rutter, M. and Quinton, D. (1984) 'Long term follow-up of women institutionalized in childhood: factors promoting good functioning in adult life', *British Journal of Developmental Psychology*, 18.

Stainton Rogers, R. and Stainton Rogers, W. (1992) *Stories of Childhood*, London: Wheatsheaf Harvester.

Williams, A.E. (1943) *Barnardo of Stepney: the father of nobody's children*, London: Allen and Unwin.

Wills, D. (1971) *Spare the Child*, Harmondsworth: Penguin.

Wilson, A. (1966) 'Convocation lecture', in *National Children's Homes, 1954–1957*, vol. 3, Chives.

Tina Herring
Freelance Writer

PART 3

WORKERS TALKING

25

Fostering Young People

In this chapter a foster carer talks about her experiences of working with young women.

Marie has been a foster carer for seven years now. She was in her early fifties when she began fostering. With her own children grown up and living away from home, and although she had a good job and was involved in voluntary work, she felt she had something more to offer, particularly to young women who were struggling with their teenage years.

Since becoming approved as a carer by a local authority, Marie has offered a home to 28 different young women. She has three 'places' at any one time but prefers to use two of these places for young women who need or want to stay for some time. The other place is often offered, on an emergency basis, to young women who either have been subject to an emergency protection order or have needed to be accommodated by the local authority at short notice.

So far the young women have all been in the 13–18 age group and have come to Marie with a wide range of issues and difficulties that have led to them being unable to stay at home. Some have been right through the care system and have not lived with their birth parents from a very early age, but instead have been moved around between children's homes, residential schools, short-term foster carers, trial periods with relatives, living on the streets and even 'secure' units. Others have been struggling at home for some time, perhaps dealing with conflict with parents about their lifestyle. Yet others have experienced sexual abuse, either recently or in the past, and may have been moved out of their home very swiftly.

Most of these young women come to Marie at a point when they might normally be planning and preparing for their futures. For them, this process has been disrupted and often they are having to deal with a traumatic present and a past that makes looking ahead difficult. However, it is essential that they do so. Local authorities only have a duty to provide services to young people until they reach 18. There is an expectation now, following the recommendations of the Children Act 1989, that support and consideration of needs of young people who have been in the care system are reviewed until they are 21. But in reality, provision varies from area to area, and many young people are left very vulnerable at the end of their time 'in care'.

It was this issue that I talked to Marie about. Nearly all the young women she has worked with have had to 'prepare' to leave care as they do not have families they can return to or depend on to help them make the transition to adulthood. How much support do these young women get? What is the role of foster carers in this situation? How much training and support do foster carers get to prepare them to deal with these issues?

> The first time I had to deal with this [leaving care] was with the first young woman I ever looked after. She had been with me nearly 18 months and we were very close. We'd worked out a very good relationship – so much so, that we very rarely needed the support of the social worker involved. This felt good at the time, but had its down side when we began to think about Halina's future. I had always known that the fostering arrangement would stop as soon as she was 18 and we'd also known she would be helped in finding a flat. Of course, there were formal reviews held which was where plans were made but there was such a huge difference between the filling in forms part of preparing for Halina to move and what actually happened.

I was interested in what the difference was.

> Well, everything was reasonably under control in relation to getting her this flat but no one seemed to pay any attention to its suitability, what kind of state it was in, or how Halina was going to set about putting it to rights.

What did you end up doing about this?

> I just couldn't let Halina go into this place in the state it was in. I ended up having her stay at mine for several more months after her 18th birthday so that we would have a chance to do some work on the flat. It wasn't just a matter of decorating either; there was black fungi on the walls, and the place was absolutely filthy. I didn't get any fostering allowance for Halina during this time. I didn't mind in one way because I cared a great deal for Halina and was only doing what any decent person would do, but I also thought it was a bit of a cheek getting

foster carers to do this kind of thing. I also lent Halina just about all the spare cash I had so she could get set up in the flat. Social services do provide a leaving care grant but it just didn't get sorted in enough time – neither did her benefits or her earnings from her job. I'll give Halina her due – she'd got herself sorted with a job and was working very hard but she just didn't know about getting herself on budgeting schemes for her electric or even really know things like needing a TV licence. I helped her sort all these things out.

Was this the end of it then?

No, not at all. And I want to stress I wouldn't want it to have been. I care very much for Halina, still do, and I'm glad to still be there for her. She comes home to me about once a week, always rings if she needs a chat, knows she can stay here if she's ill or a bit down. I've also done other things; nothing to blow a trumpet about, just things you would do as a parent. Things like make a party for her on her 21st – yes! she's that old now! And also look over her boyfriends when she's met someone new, and other practical things. As I said, she's very organised now but there is always some time when she needs a loan of a pound or two.

Surely you don't do this for all the other 27 young women?

Well, no, I couldn't possibly. Maybe Halina was a bit special being the first, but I also had to realise my limitations. I hadn't had any training as such around this issue until after Halina left me but following that I insisted. My link worker in the fostering team invited me to attend a conference about young people leaving care and I realised that I would have to be very aware of my limitations in future; perhaps put more energy next time in preparation *before* the young person left and also, I hate to say it, in putting back some of these responsibilities to the social worker.

What sort of changes have you made in the way you work with these young women in relation to them leaving your and the local authority's care then?

I'm much better planned and much more demanding! For example, I now do things like encourage the young women to learn to budget – even at an early age, say 14, I have them come shopping with me and see how much things cost and also help them take responsibility for things like their clothes allowance. When they are a bit older they are asked to make a meal once a week, on a certain budget. I don't make it seem like work I don't think – much more about taking responsibility and relating that to freedoms you have alongside that. It's also something about being together as a group of women – learning to live and work together and having respect for each other. And that very much includes me! And as I said, I'm also much more demanding of social workers – I recognise the time everything takes so I make sure they start planning for things like flats, leaving care grants etc. in plenty of time.

Apart from budgeting and cooking I was also interested in her comment about living together as a group of women.

> I suppose it's something to do with why I do this job, and about what I believe in. I come from a very large, East End working class family, with very traditional roles. It was also a family where there was male violence and complete male domination. It was not an easy way to grow up and it took me a long time to become strong in myself. I've always benefited enormously from my friendships with women and I've got great belief in women being strong and able in this world. An awful lot of the young women who come to me have been abused in one way or another. They certainly come with a low opinion of themselves and are often deeply mistrusting of almost everyone. Also, many seem more dependent on boyfriends (who also often don't treat them too well) than they are on their women friends. I suppose I want to create not only an atmosphere where as four women we can respect and trust each other, but most importantly an atmosphere where everyone can feel safe. I also believe they will benefit from having friends and relationships to fall back on when they leave me to go into flats or hostels or even into living with their boyfriends, having kids, whatever.

So how important is the issue of personal safety?

> Oh yes, most definitely. I'm very clear about boundaries in the household. Both practical ones like locking doors, not letting strangers into the house, being careful who you give your address to, and also boundaries about things like ending up at someone else's house without any money to get home, going off in cars with men you don't know very well at all, inviting men into your flat when you get it. It's not that I'm against men at all. In fact, one of the positive things that happens here is the Sunday lunch. On these occasions we all get to invite someone over and the young women therefore meet a wide variety of people – male, female, young and old – and they learn to both respect and be respected in social situations. This is also a time when young women invite their family members so they, too, can become part of the set-up in a safe way. It's much more about helping young women see that there is good and bad in everything and everyone but that they can be vulnerable with men. I hope they learn to feel good enough about themselves so that they won't put up with bad treatment. That's the sort of safety that means the most to me.

But what are the difficulties?

> There have been quite a few that just haven't settled or who I just couldn't reach. One young woman was a firestarter and I was so worried about this and other very damaging behaviour that I ended up not feeling I could let her out of my sight. I just couldn't cope with the fear of something terrible being just about to happen. When she did actually start a fire it was the end. She had to go. I couldn't protect the other girls and look after her. It still makes me enormously sad but what she needed was more than I could offer. She needed some kind of place with 24-hour supervision but most of all 24-hour help and

specialist therapy. Another girl I couldn't work with because she just couldn't get off drugs. She was stealing and just unreachable. She was involved in doing things that I just couldn't cope with – like stealing from old people. She just radiated hate. It was too destructive for us all. It's not like the others have been angels either! I've had property damaged, money stolen, things stolen. I've been accused (wrongly and thankfully I could prove it!), I've had young people run away and I've been mad with worry. I've had young people come back obviously well under the influence. I've been up all night dealing with the police and I've had countless hours counselling the parents of young people [a major part of the job, often not realised, is to help keep lines of communication going with parents].

And that makes it sound so negative! Why do you do it, Marie?

It's a challenge. I actually enjoy young people because it makes me feel I've got something to give from my own difficult life experiences, I've got so much energy, I wouldn't know what to do with it all and I'm 61 this year. I like being a strong woman working to support this in others. I think I'll still be doing it when I'm 80 – if they'll let me!

Interview by Val Williams
Barnardo's

26

The Teacher's Story

Rob Morrish has taught science at the same school since September 1972. In the succeeding 24 years he has seen significant shifts not only in teaching practice and the running of the school, but also in the demands placed upon both teachers and pupils. Here he talks about his experiences over these changing times.

Did you have an idea of your 'role' when you first went into teaching?

> Not at all really. To be fair, I had studied educational history and educational psychology, sociology and philosophy at college, but I think although I had thought about it very deeply it was still very abstract and I hadn't done a lot of actual practical stuff. When you get into the real job it's very different to doing it in theory.

Is that the same now?

> I dunno, I think it's even worse now probably. People I've spoken to who've come into education since me seem to do a lot less studying of those types of things. I think pragmatically they're much better prepared, but I don't know if they're as prepared philosophically.
>
> I hoped, when I first went into education, to see myself a lot more as a facilitator than as being merely didactic. I was a bit starry-eyed I think. I joined a boys' secondary modern school in the year that the school leaving age went up. The very first lesson I ever taught was a bunch of final year lads just expecting to leave, who were told that they had to stay on for another year. So you can imagine what they were like. There I was standing at the front thinking I was going to be this facilitator helping them to do what they wanted to do, and they didn't want to do anything. Well, there was no point facilitating them to do that! So I had to take on more of a didactic role than I had hoped.

So have you ever found it possible to be a facilitator?

> Yes, later on I have. But I think you need more skills. You need more experience to be able to do it. Obviously it depends on the kids as well. I was going to say 'if you get a bunch of well-motivated kids', but it's partly up to you to motivate them. It works two ways, but when everything comes together and things go well, then yes, you can facilitate.

Has the National Curriculum affected this in any way?

It depends on which specific schools and which specific kids you're talking about.

Since science has been modularised I have been able to run some experimental courses, but if we go back historically to when I first started and it was a secondary modern school of 400 boys, in a year of 80 boys only the top stream of about a dozen were entered for CSE exams – and they were all entered for CSE physics. Maybe one or two who had a specific interest may have done biology, but there were only two science staff and one laboratory.

And the equipment that we had was non-existent. I remember having to ask the boys to bring in jam jars for experiments because we couldn't afford beakers or conical flasks.

By the way, the other 60-odd boys who weren't sitting physics did non-examination science, and basically that was whatever you wanted it to be.

Nowadays, every child does science, and does general science which includes some aspects that we would never have touched: geological stuff, science relating to the environment, and information technology.

There is so much more expectation today. A lot's asked of them, which is good in a way; gone are the days when kids could leave school not knowing how to wire a plug, or not knowing about their own bodies, or the impacts of chemical pollution.

What pressure have this expansion and the National Curriculum put on teachers?

The bugbear of the National Curriculum is that it has changed so many times. It's got to have changed four or five times in science, and every time we write our own schemes of work; it gets to be a bit of a bind when two years later you've got to write them all again. That's not something that's gone down too well.

But I don't know many teachers who are against the National Curriculum itself. Kids leave school having done a good, wide grounding in things. It's opened up education to be much more broad than it was.

Do you think these constant changes have had a negative effect on the kids at all?

I don't think so really. The staff sometimes get a bit cheesed off when they've got to rewrite things, but I don't think it's affected the kids. When you're in the classroom you teach what you've got to teach.

So how do you feel when you hear the government saying that standards have dropped?

Well, for a start-off, I definitely do not accept that standards have dropped. I think when you see what's expected of kids nowadays, and what they have to do – eight modular tests over two years, practical experiments, their final written exam, and they've got to average, say,

40% over all that work – you cannot say that standards have dropped. In fact I think the kids do very well to cope with it.

One of the old clichés used to criticise education is that you can't apply the stuff you learnt to life outside the classroom. How do you respond to that?

Again, I think that's something we have improved. I remember one of the old chemistry questions was: 'Discuss the reactions in the blast furnace – 30 marks.' A thing like that was no good to anybody! The questions now are related to everyday life and put into context. Kids will have done experiments on chemistry in the kitchen, chemistry in cooking. Stuff like that.

Do you still see the preparation of kids for life after school as being the role of a teacher?

Those unseen pedagogical practices have always gone on. But I think that's been formalised a lot more than it used to be. In our school we have an hour's tutor period specifically set aside every week. We try and touch on things like racism, sexism, and health education. And being formalised, it's more recognised. Again, this is a good thing, because in times gone by, even on the academic side of things, you were leaving a lot more to chance than you do now.

Kids can come and see you outside of session times as well, because they will find informal pathways if they need to, whether it's because they don't like their specific form teacher, or because of the nature of their problem or whatever. In the past I've dealt with a kid who had one of their parents commit suicide, and I've had a kid who had to be taken into care because of abuse. Thankfully, in the end, she got through that, but you do have to guard against the kids who feel there isn't anyone there for them to talk to. That is another reason why the formal session is a good idea, but kids have always gone to their teachers.

Is that an aspect of teaching that you think is overlooked in training or people's expectations of the role?

I don't think there can be many teachers in the profession 25 years who've never had a kid approach them with problems. But yeah, I think when people get involved in a bit of teacher-bashing it is something that they overlook. There are some who'd say it's not our job – and some parts aren't. If they get too hairy then you do have to pass them on to other agencies. But sometimes kids will specifically ask you not to do that. They won't come and talk to you if they think that's going to happen. You have to walk a bit of a tightrope from time to time. And you can be sure it isn't easy.

Again, when I think back, I was lucky because I took a year out about 10 years ago to do my master's degree and within that I did do a counselling course. There are lots of teachers that don't get that. I think it would be a good idea, if it can be afforded, to give any teacher who has taught, say, 20 years, a year off in order to go out and learn some new things; just recharge their batteries. I found that year off did me tremendous good. It opened my eyes.

Interview by Daren Garratt
The Open University

27

The Youth Worker's Account

I first met Phil Creed in 1988 when my band played at the youth centre that he ran. Over the next few years, we turned an exhausted youth club into a reputable youth arts centre, live venue and recording studio, attracting national and international artists. I say 'we' because although Phil was the worker there, he was never a leader, more a catalyst through which our projects could be realised. Like many radical departures, it encountered problems and criticism, until eventually it had to be wound down. This is Phil's story.

When I was about 19 in the early seventies, I was quite keenly evangelical, and I got involved with the West End council churches in Edinburgh. They ran a club called Charisma which was set up in a crypt under one of the churches. I did that as a volunteer.

Although the club wasn't *madly* evangelical, I felt increasingly frustrated finding that consoling people with a chapter from the Bible just wasn't enough. Anyway, one night a friend asked me if I'd thought of training for a *career in youth work,* which amazed me! I didn't know there was such a job as paid youth work. Few people do even now.

So, was your motivation largely religious?

Not really, 'cos by the time I'd done my training I'd spent some time in London and I guess I started to question my religious beliefs and looked for other values to fill that vacuum. It was an education, and what motivates me, as both a youth worker and an individual, is to a large extent the educational value that I think the job has. And by education I don't mean schooling, but the ability and eagerness to learn. For me, what is most rewarding about the job is the chance to learn new things.

Is that an ideal you've been able to put into practice?

Well, when I moved to my present post in 1985, I got a sense that things were very different to other youth centres I'd been involved in. It was becoming harder to interest people in projects.

But hasn't that become the problem with youth clubs generally, and the stereotypes they suggest?

The stereotype of the youth club has become self-perpetuating. What would have been the 'tick-over' mechanisms of a club – like pool or table tennis – have become the core. They're the only things on the programme, and rather than go out and try and identify the needs of the current generation of young people, we've said, 'Well, this is what we've got in the building, so this is what we're stuck with, so this is what we've got to offer.'

I could see that if something wasn't done, the place would just die on its feet. I felt that it needed some research to find out why kids weren't going to the centre, so we devised a questionnaire of 200 questions and went onto the street.

We discovered, firstly, that young people want to do things for themselves more. Be awarded more independence. We also found that they wanted the opportunity to do more specialised things. In other words, they wanted to junk the 'dossing around' image of the youth club, and have the resources to be more positive.

How did you capitalise upon these findings?

I knew we had to actually reject what they were rejecting and start again with some jointly worked out idea. It was quite a radical move and pretty scary. But, I think the key thing for me wasn't to make it provisions-based. Instead of saying '*We* have decided that we will provide you with a recording studio', it was more a case of, 'We are open to working with you and supporting *your* projects.'

So the thing grew more organically. It was secure. And *relevant*. People were working things out for themselves rather than just getting along with things they were provided with. And, in the more general scheme of things, I think what was crucial was that we were offering experiential modes.

What do you mean?

If you envisage a youth club as a way of trying out some of the set structures of adult society, well, with the centre I wanted to create a variety of organisational models, with differing political or social principles. Whether collectivist or entrepreneurial it didn't matter. I felt that regardless of a young person's political stance, they should be comfortable in one of a number of organisations within the centre, and learn something about themselves through those organisations.

How did other youth workers react to this approach?

Well, I felt that I was researching new approaches which might be transferable to other centres, so it frustrated me when I had colleagues saying, 'Oh, he's not doing proper youth work.' But a regular Saturday night gigs programme would attract 100+ people, and the skills training involved in a group of young people organising that was crucially important. It would have fallen flat on its face if the groundwork hadn't been done. It was a very stable, positive environment which a lot of people got encouragement and help from, but generally it wasn't seen as valuable youth work. More like an eccentric hobby.

That's really sad. I'm surprised other local youth centres didn't follow your lead, or get involved with you more.

Actually, there was a youth centre up the road, within walking distance, that has got a proper sports hall, and I went through a period where I tried to persuade them to twin with us. Y'know, they'd specialise in sports, we'd specialise more in the arts, and we'd programme jointly.

Did that work?

No. They didn't want to know.

So is this the end of the youth club as we know it?

Most council-run youth centres were built over 20 years ago. In the interim there have been a lot of social changes that have heightened the opportunity for kids to have more privacy *in their own rooms*. This has increasingly meant that purpose-built youth clubs that were very busy and relevant in their first 10 years of existence, have become almost irrelevant to the vast majority of young people.

Since the gig programme folded our centre's become dead again, but I'm no longer convinced that there are huge numbers of kids on the streets at any given time. So, instead of trying to refill these old buildings, I think we should provide something like Portakabins, that you could just give these kids the keys to – not completely abandon it to them, but give them the opportunity to run this thing for themselves. Give them a meeting place. Provide a support worker who'll meet them every so often to help resolve any social conflicts, and y'know . . . let them learn from having a bit of responsibiity, and the inevitable problems that go with it. People have to learn to be accountable.

And when that project's exhausted itself, and that community's aged, as communities do, you've got something you can shove on the back of a lorry and move somewhere else. Y'see, the dilemma is that a lot of money is being sucked into keeping these old buildings on the go, rather than budgeting for the experimental, smaller, focused work on the fringes.

You just mentioned 'communities' again. Why is it that kids come and go in cycles, but management and youth workers don't seem to?

Conventional wisdom says it's good to move every three to five years, but what's working against that is the cutbacks in council spending. Many people are scared to move, so everyone's holding onto the jobs they've got. Thus, there are fewer jobs advertised, and there's much less chance for people to grow and mature in their work. They're not getting the chance to get involved in new challenges. I'm looking for a move at the moment, and part of the reason for that is finally realising that things *do* go in cycles. As long as I'm stuck, the centre's going to be stuck. To try and create a new future in the existing setting is hard for me. It would be a lot easier to take on new challenges in a new setting. The centre will find a new direction more quickly with a fresh worker in charge of it.

Interview by Daren Garratt
The Open University

28

A Probation Officer's Tale: Working on Health

Rod Waters is a social worker in a children and families team in Taunton and lectures at a further education college. He came from a very large mining family in South Wales, has taught music in Brixton and has been an adult guidance worker.

Roger de Wolf is a probation officer in Bath and freelance trainer. He grew up in a middle class London suburb and has been a youth arts worker, stage manager and freelance photographer/journalist, and has run a mobile community development project.

Here they look at the issues raised in setting up and running a health group for young men.

Young men's health continues to be a surprisingly neglected area of concern, despite increasing knowledge about it. This can be seen as part of a general attitude of dismissiveness towards the vulnerability and developmental needs of young men. They are increasingly seen not to have problems, but to be the problem.

For two decades we have each had a deepening interest in issues of 'masculinity'. We have very different class origins and career paths. The strength of our shared ideas and the difference of our life experiences have enabled us to explore the changing patterns of masculinities in post-industrial Britain.

Here we look at some of the ways in which our work with a group of men from a small industrial town in Somerset has raised our awareness of health issues and has informed our practice in working with young men.

Some of the young men in our group had mental health problems, and most lacked confidence and self-esteem owing to poor literacy, social isolation, poverty or learning disabilities. Their social opportunities were often blighted in a town noted for its hard drinking and violence.

In addition to these obvious disadvantages, it also became painfully apparent that all group members were survivors of childhood abuse or neglect. Their concept of conflict resolution was largely limited to the commission of or submission to acts of violence.

Inevitably, in such a small community, many group members knew and understood each other's backgrounds. However in the early days of our work together we observed that this commonality of experience was rarely openly acknowledged. In fact the group dynamic ensured that it was routinely suppressed, as was any admission of difficulty, sorrow or pain. The only strong emotions allowed by the group were humour (so often misplaced), fear and anger.

We would like to pay tribute to the vision of the community education development workers who perceived a need and took pioneering action to fund and start a group for men in Somerset, when this was still a ground-breaking idea in cities. The notion was current, and is in many places still, that men do not need support, and that working with 'gender issues' means working with women. The local probation team, for example, rejected the idea of working in groups with men as being inherently sexist, while advertising support groups for women. They seemed to neglect or actively reject the opportunity of tackling gender issues in the groups they ran, ignoring the fact that these groups often comprised men only.

In the early stage of our working partnership we lacked appropriate support and supervision. Exploring the hidden and fragile complexity of other men's issues in such a setting, with no space in which to deal with our own, we were thrown very much on each other, and often felt almost conspiratorial. We were uncomfortably aware of this, and of the dangers of colluding in sexism and the abuse of power. We found it very difficult to clearly review our practice. Consequently, it took us a painfully long time to recognise that we had inherited some ineffective working methods. The group had not been constructed as a support or discussion group, although it had been given this title. It resembled an adult guidance and social club with optional one-to-one counselling. Evenings generally featured checking out local job adverts, community news, pool and darts, advice and general conversation over unending cups of tea and coffee. Sometimes a member would ask a worker for a private word upstairs, or a one-to-one session would be initiated by us if someone behaved angrily or disruptively. As we had both been trained in person-centred counselling, it seemed natural to continue offering this individual facility. We did not recognise that in doing so we were damaging the group process. We were colluding in keeping feelings of vulnerability or weakness private, behind the counselling room door. The confidentiality of a counselling contract only served to help members put their 'masculine mask' back on before returning to the group, reinforcing many of the barriers between these men. It was apparent that we therefore colluded in their isolation and power-lessness.

We had trapped ourselves into a rigid routine which did not allow the group to grow. Recognising the need for change, we sought group work consultancy and appropriate supervision. We planned a huge shift towards a more empowering and process-based model of group work, starting during the preparation for a weekend residential. This presented an ideal opportunity for us to enable 10 young men to take responsibility for themselves and their decision making. Despite enormous resistance and many teething problems, we insisted that all issues were referred back to the entire group. Whatever the task (budgeting, cooking, etc.), our focus was always on process: discussion, co-operation, fairness, etc. Individual sessions were no longer on offer, and for the first time, personal difficulties were shared and explored and conflicts openly recognised. This was a success, owing to our determina-tion, to the strong relationships of trust which we had with members, to the extended time that the group shared and to the group's enormous excitement at being together so far from home (for some members this was their first journey away from Somerset). We found it moving, to an almost magical extent, to watch these men, most of whom had never experienced male warmth, care, or positive regard, discovering the possibility and the deep pleasure of caring for each other.

Following the residential, the shift in emphasis was built into the structure of group evenings. Games and socialising were still included, but time was set aside for whole group discussions, planning and decision making. As workers we were consciously beginning the careful process of handing over power and control of the group to its membership. Members welcomed and thrived on the change, having now established the necessary confidence to explore more and more difficult subjects in the whole group. Individual counselling was discontinued.

In the growing atmosphere of trust and care, issues previously only revealed in the counselling room were now tentatively shared and tested with the group. Health matters, whether physical or mental, became a common recurring theme. It was obvious that many group members had never had an opportunity to discuss their fears and doubts about their health before, and they were alarmingly ignorant about all aspects of sexuality. We aimed to empower the group to learn by providing neutral or friendly sources of information (for example, *Everyman* by Derek Llewel-lyn-Jones). Ignorance was not stigmatised but seen as a learning opportunity for all of us. The 'It's a Man's World' board game was a popular and safe way to begin the process of exploring and sharing information and sounding out attitudes.

We found that very few of the men remembered ever having had a medical check-up. In common with so many men, they seemed not to expect to be cared for in this way, and it was a point of macho pride to be able to do without it. For men in most areas of the country there is no male equivalent of the well-woman clinic, and they often feel excluded from caring community resources such as family planning clinics, health centres and family centres. It is now recognised that young men are hugely more at risk of falling victim to violent crime than any other group of the population, and that the young male suicide rate is rising alarmingly.

We had always checked out group members' health during counselling sessions, but this was a private, worker-led process. They had now taken permission to voice their own health concerns and share them with the whole group, feeling that they had a right to be listened to.

As the group's health consciousness grew, members became visibly more able to care for themselves, and therefore able to express their care for each other. A genuine concern for the mental health problems of one member replaced ridicule. The group became aware of the pain and tragic disintegration of another member through Huntington's chorea, and felt able to support him with the affectionate consideration he needed in order to maintain his dignity.

Working on health matters with this group of young men was important in itself. It was also a vehicle for, and an organic part of, a wider process of growth and empowerment for men who had previously learned that it was 'manly' to repress any real concern for themselves or each other.

Rod Waters
Social Worker

Roger de Wolf
Probation Officer

29

The Residential Social Worker's Tale

Here two women talk about the changes in practice they have experienced in their years of working with young people.

Eleanor and Rachael are black women who work in a residential setting with young people age 16 and over. They are both experienced care workers: Eleanor has worked in residential settings for over six years, working with children and young people from 6 to 21, and Rachael has worked in children's homes, residential settings with young people and as a foster carer. They met with me to talk about how practice has changed since they first started in social work and whether they consider the changes to be positive.

I first asked how they had got involved in residential social work. Eleanor replied:

> A lot of my family have worked in the care field, both in this country and others. It's always been a topic of conversation in the household and I guess I picked up both an interest at an early age and some knowledge and understanding. It seemed natural to go into this kind of work myself.

Rachael added:

> It was much the same for me. The family talked a lot about care work. It always felt that it would be a good area to go into. I felt comfortable with it.

I wanted to know what their first experiences were like, particularly in relation to how they were trained or taught to do the work. They both laughed and Eleanor went on to say:

> I had no training before I started, but as I said, the work seemed fairly natural to me. I did have a lot of support, too. It was like learning on the job. I shadowed a social worker for some time but even with this there were often times I had to do what I believed to be best. I needed to be able to make decisions fairly early on. The young people were constantly testing me out. I think I was quite firm and fairly confident though, which helped. I think they knew where they were with me. I was also very committed to offering a good service, particularly with young black people whose needs I really thought were being neglected.

Rachael nodded in agreement and went on to say:

> Yes, that was a big issue for me, too. There seemed to be absolutely no attention paid to the needs of young black people. It was just ignored. I don't think anyone meant it to be this way, I think they thought it better to ignore differences. That meant that all the issues young black people were facing might just go away. They also seemed to think that it was racist even to consider that there was a difference.

I asked then if they, as black workers, felt responsible for taking the needs of young black people into account rather than this being shared. Eleanor said:

> Definitely. Good practice seemed to be promoted by the black workers only and not the responsibility of anyone else. It was just left to us to sort out these issues and deal with what the young black residents might be experiencing. There was a huge lack of awareness about things like young black men constantly being picked up by the police, or the racism that a young woman was experiencing at school.

Rachael continued:

> And it was other things, too, like never looking at the strengths of black families but instead almost taking it for granted that young black people were in care, as if family life wasn't positive for them. I'm sure that attitude led to many more young black people not ever going home again. There was a real reluctance from the staff to engage with the parents. It was also something about how little the actual residential unit resembled home and how there was never anything provided that validated what the parents' lifestyle was; for example, a different religious perspective or different family values. I know some of that has changed now, and for the better.

I asked what she meant. She replied:

> Well, I really think the Children Act has made a big difference. It's now down on paper, the word of the law so to speak. You have to take into account the race, religion, culture and language of a child or young person. I really think that has made a big difference. And now it's in nearly everything – all the forms you get from social services, child care reviews, care plans. Nearly all the work has to consider, at least on paper, how this is being dealt with.

Has that affected everybody's practice, I wondered. Rachael said:

> I do think it's made a difference. All workers do seem to think more about it and when they're up against any opposition, they can quote the Act. It feels more to me that we share the responsibility for the issue. Although I don't think the issues can ever be the same for white workers. I think I do it from the heart, not because it's in a bit of legislation. And it is easy to make a mockery of it. For example, thinking all black people are the same and therefore I can voice *the* black perspective rather than *a* black perspective. There's a long way

to go yet, but the Act's definitely helped. Another thing that's vital is recognising that black workers can offer more than just work with black young people.

Eleanor added:

As a black care worker I do see the needs of a black service user initially, but the focus of my work is to see the needs of young people as a whole. That's very important to me.

I was interested in what other practice had changed following the Children Act. Eleanor said:

Another major part of the Children Act is the guidance around working with the age group we work with now – the young people who are 16 or over. We find that difficult to work with. It shows up some of the limitations of legislation really. Although young people are still, in the law's eyes, children until they are 18, if they have been 'accommodated', the new term for voluntary care, after their 16th birthday, the duties of the local authority are a bit different. And I would say less rather than just different. They could end up in bed and breakfast rather than with a carer, or even in a homeless hostel. Also, if they are over 18 it changes again. The local authority should befriend and assist but the responsibility to actually provide is minimal. It's incredibly hard for young people of this age to find a way into the system and then round it so that they get something of what they need.

Rachael went on:

It's particularly hard when you're working with a young person who is disallowed a service just because of their age. For example, we've just been fighting with a local authority about a young woman who's 18 in terms of her age, but emotionally she's much younger. She's also just disclosed she was sexually abused as a child and she's extremely vulnerable. Our service would be able to continue to work with her by offering her supported accommodation with other young people and the care and support of staff. However, because of her age, her local authority are refusing to pay the necessary fees and have only agreed to four weeks of what we call 'outreach' – that is, to have a member of staff support her in her own accommodation for this limited spell. We can see that this will not be enough. And it's all prescribed by age!

I wanted to explore how the service drew the line between offering support and being over-protective. After all, many young people of this sort of age group cope very well without intervention. Eleanor continued:

It's something to do with the way I think we work here. And that's another thing that's changed over the past few years. We used to joke that all we offered was a babysitting service. We provided accommodation and not much else really. That's changed so much. We now work very much *with* the young people; for example, no one stays here unless they want to. We work very much on what they want out of being here, how they want to lead their lives, what they want to achieve. Now that's not traditional residential care, is it! We also are much better at supporting a young person in their family life, however difficult that is. I don't think we could be accused of being over-protective but yes, we do offer care and concern. Let's face it, who of us didn't need some support and help in that spell between being a child, then adolescent, then young adult? I certainly did. Care leavers now are just pushed into society and the ones we work with have often had really difficult lives to deal with as well.

It sounded so different from the 'children's homes' of the past, so I asked what else had prompted the changes, apart from the Children Act. Rachael answered:

I think something has changed about how we value young people. I think we were taught to think of them as kind of enemies at one point and they had to be controlled and managed somehow. Don't get me wrong, we still have to deal with challenging behaviour but something has moved in our basic philosophy. It used to be an 'us and them' situation where you didn't really get involved unless you had to. Now we do, but with boundaries. We're clear, mostly, about getting alongside a young person, finding out what they want and supporting them and enabling them to do it themselves. It's something to do with respect. I also think it actually works better. It's certainly made the job I do now much better than I did six years ago – better for me and for the young person.

Eleanor concluded the interview by saying:

Yes, a lot has changed – mostly for the good with the different atti-tudes and ways of working – but we haven't got it all right yet. Like I said, I think resources for some young people in this age group can be really poor. We still want young people to be adults when it suits us, as with parts of the Children Act that demand we take their wishes and feelings into account. But we also don't want to empower young people to make decisions and choices for themselves, for example in legislation around voting, sexual freedoms and marriage. And we adults associate adolescents with confusion. I think it's us!

Interview by Val Williams
Barnardo's

30

The GP's Account

Here a GP provides an account of the kinds of health issues affecting young people that she deals with. All names have been changed.

This chapter is specifically about the problems that are presented to the GP by young people aged 11–20. As a general statement the work of a GP is geared towards the old and the under-5s and we probably don't see a great deal of 11–20 year olds. They are mostly healthy and getting on with their lives and don't want to spend time coming to the doctor.

Most health problems, that is minor day-to-day symptoms such as coughs, colds, minor injuries, are dealt with by people themselves and are not presented to the GP. When people do present to the GP something has made them anxious about their symptoms and they seek reassurance or treatment. One of the most rewarding aspects of being a GP is that most of the time you can confidently give reassurance that a symptom presented (such as headaches) is easily dealt with and not as serious as the person feared (in this case, a brain tumour). Often young people will come seeking reassurance and knowledge about the significance of minor symptoms. Sometimes they find it difficult to express what their real fear is and it takes time in the consultation to find out exactly why the person came.

The problem with young people . . .

I thought I would describe some of the more specific problems faced by young people who present to the GP and then talk specifically about a few case histories.

The major physical change of the ages 11–20 of course is puberty. Interestingly the physical changes at puberty seem to proceed straightforwardly for the vast majority and people rarely come to the GP with problems associated with puberty. Injuries and fractures are common in this age group, related to sport, but they are usually dealt with by hospital casualty departments.

The other sorts of problems that young people of this age sometimes have are somatisation of psychological distress either at home or at school: for example, headaches, abdominal pain. Parents bring the young person, not because they think they have some serious disease, but because the symptoms – abdominal pain and headaches – are leading to time off school or behavioural difficulties at home. This sort of presentation can be difficult. Sometimes, as before, reassurance about the physical symptoms may be all that is required and then the parent or young person will have the confidence to deal with the problem themselves.

Often the situation is more complex and may involve multiple consultations with different members of the family, together and separately, to get to the root of the problem. Sometimes one will see a young person and his or her family for a spell with this sort of consultation and then they disappear and you don't see them for years. Usually I expect this means that the situation has got better just with the process of time. As GPs we are often just voyeurs on the stages of people's lives and don't always know what the beginning or the end of the story is.

Young people aged 14–20 appear more frequently in the surgery than their younger counterparts. Here the problems are more varied and encompass a vast array of problems from acne to complex issues such as pregnancy, avoidance of pregnancy, termination of pregnancy, drugs, depression, major mental illness, sexual problems, sexually transmitted disease, eating disorders, stress related to exams, stress related to employment or lack of it, conflict with parents, and problems related to being young and poor and being parents, either singly or in a couple.

A day in the life

I thought I might try to illustrate some of these descriptions with some typical cases, all of which might commonly be presented in the surgery.

Amanda is 15. Since she and her family registered with us two years ago, she has been a frequent attender in the surgery. She comes on her own. She is one of four girls, her mum is a single parent. In the two-year period we have seen her she has changed in appearance from being a puffy, pale-faced adolescent to a young woman. She comes to open surgeries (that is, without an appointment), sits for ages, missing school while waiting to be seen. When she comes in she presents a physical problem, headache, abdominal pains, vaginal itching, backache etc. She is shy and reserved. Examination never reveals any cause for symptoms. On questioning she denies any worries or stresses. I ask if there is something she wants to talk about, perhaps school, home, boyfriends, contraception. But I never get anywhere. In the meantime we might discuss her diet, which might be causing constipation, which might be causing abdominal pain (she lives on pot noodles). I make it clear I am happy to talk about contraception, drugs, so perhaps some health education goes on in the interview, but I am left feeling dissatisfied. I don't know why she has come, perhaps I never will. I have seen a lot of Amanda but I know very little about her. GPs think they know their patients well, but I have come to the view that we know very little about them. We know what they tell us; often that gives us a window into their lives through which we project our own prejudices and fantasies which can give a very distorted view.

Finally one day Amanda came to the surgery and asked me if I believed in SAD (seasonal affective disorder). I asked her how she'd heard about it: she'd read about it in a magazine. 'Aha, at last,' I thought, 'we're going to get somewhere.' She then agreed that she'd been feeling mildly depressed but didn't know why. I then jumped in at the deep end by suggesting that I refer her to a specialist adolescent service where they have trained counsellors who have the time and experience to talk to young people. She seemed to go along with this. I made the appointment for her, but she didn't keep it. Had I scared her off by referring to a specialist service? After all these consultations about physical symptoms she'd finally had the courage to ask me about SAD: had I let her down by suggesting that I pass her on to someone else? But I haven't the time or the expertise to do in-depth counselling. I haven't seen her since that last consultation. I am sure I will. That's the thing about general practice, you usually get another chance to take things a little bit further.

Three women and their babies

Nasreen is 19, she is now 18 weeks pregnant. Regularly for the next six months she will be coming to the surgery for antenatal checks. On the few occasions I have seen her so far, she has come accompanied by her mother-in-law. She looks a little sad. She is a second generation Pakistani woman, brought up in the Midlands. She has come to the North because of her marriage. She speaks perfect English, having lived here all her life and briefly had a job when she left school. She knows now her life is to be at home and have children. She lives in a small flat with her husband's parents. I wonder what it is like for her. I know she misses her family in the Midlands very much. Over the next few years I will probably see a lot of her and her babies and I look forward to this and the fact that we will be able to communicate as we have our language in common.

It is the end of a surgery; the receptionist asks if I would like to see an extra who has just registered as a temporary patient. In comes Mary, who is 18, with her one and a half year old boy who has cut his finger. The injury is not serious, he had trapped his finger in a door. The account of how it happened fits with the injury. The child has no other bruises, or signs of neglect or abuse. Mary is harassed and agitated. She is in a bed and breakfast nearby, having left the boy's father who was violent to her. He has found where she is and is harassing her. I suggest that she goes to Women's Aid, but she doesn't like the idea of Women's Aid. She is waiting for the council to rehouse her and wants it now. She is also angry with her own mother, whom she feels doesn't help her enough, despite the fact that she spends most of her days at her mother's house. I ask how old her mother is: 38 was the reply. Mary leaves, I can't help her with her housing, I may never see her again and she may be rehoused away from the surgery.

Now a house visit request to a child with a cough. The mother, Sharon, is also 18. She is very anxious. Sharon suffers acute anxiety and is a multiple user of the doctor. She was sexually abused herself as a child. Sharon looks terrified and anxious, she walks up and down wringing her hands in despair. She can barely cope. She lives with the boy's father, Pedro, who is Spanish. She speaks no Spanish, he speaks poor English. They both seem devoted to the child, but have huge problems communicating with each other. Sharon is reassured that the baby's cough is not serious. We talk about her worries as all the time she paces the floor, wringing her hands. She is actually a bit better than she was six months ago when she first registered. Regular visits from the health visitor and a full-time nursery place for the baby are helping her cope. She really wants to make a good job of being a parent.

You may feel that I am concentrating a lot on the problems of young women who are mothers, but they are a group of young women whom I see a lot of. Motherhood is definitely an option for some young women, it is something they can achieve in a society where they can achieve little else. They do so at a cost to themselves of loss of their own youth and acquire responsibilities and problems which seem never ending.

The bitterest pill

Other young people with jobs, pursuing careers etc. don't come much to the doctor. When they do they come for pill prescriptions.

They are often clear about what they want. It doesn't mean they don't have problems, but perhaps they have more resources among themselves and their friends to cope with them. They will have crises, perhaps an unwanted pregnancy, or short-term misery about the breakup of a relationship. In our area we have very easy access for termination of pregnancy. In this age group it is often very clear to the woman that she wants a termination of pregnancy and it seems to me that, as a generalisation, there is less ambivalence than in older women. I realise I am talking more about women than men, as it is true of all ages that women consult the GP more than men.

As a gross generalisation, drugs in our practice are more of a problem for young men. Neil is 18, unemployed, has never been employed, and is a father. He hardly ever sees his infant daughter. He has been using a mixture of diazepam, temazepam, dihydrocodeine and methadone from the streets for some years. We tried to stabilise his life by giving him daily scripts for methadone in the hope that it would stop him buying drugs. The idea is that if we stabilise his life, stop him shoplifting to get money for drugs etc., he will eventually grow out of his drug need. Some people see drug dependence as a sort of prolonged adolescence. I personally feel the whole question of drug addicts being treated by GPs is a very vexed one. The GP contact with the addict is not an easy one. The GP holds the power of being able to issue a script and we use that as constructively as possible. I personally have had the experience of prescribing methadone for a patient, in this instance a woman. She then sold the methadone or gave it to a much younger boy aged 15, who died of an overdose. The drug addiction problems that we see relate mainly to temazepam, dihydrocodeine and methadone abuse, and are phenomena of very poor, deprived council estates. I expect they are rather different from the drug problems relating to the designer drugs which young people use at raves. I have very little experience of young people's use of these drugs. They don't seem to want to discuss it with the GP. It would also be fair to say that most GPs know very little about them.

GPs of course don't work in isolation, they work within the general practice team, and the health visitor and nurse are valuable resources for younger people. We also have professional contacts with many of the other people who are writing chapters for this book.

Irene Paterson
General Practitioner

31

Sexual Health

Jo is a health promotion officer, with special responsibility for working with young people. I talked to her about some of the difficulties she has experienced when talking to young people about sexual health within their school settings.

I first asked Jo about who she worked with:

> As a service we respond to any enquiries from schools, youth or community groups and any other settings working with young people in relation to education and training in areas of health and sex education, including advice and information on HIV/AIDS for young people in the 5–25 age group.

I was interested in the definition of a 'young person', so asked about the age range. Jo responded:

> The age range is defined by some aspects of law and LEA guidelines, but our service does not work with the notion that young people become adults overnight on their 18th birthday. We also have an LEA framework for over- and under-16s in relation to sex education, particularly around advice about safer sex, in terms of both HIV infection and prevention of pregnancy.

I was also interested in the content of health promotion in a school setting: I guessed it was led by more than just the legal framework of what could and couldn't be discussed. Jo affirmed this view:

> I've worked in a large number of different schools within a relatively small geographical area. Each school has wanted a different focus in relation to sexual health promotion. For example, in a local girls' school we weren't allowed to actually bring condoms with us, although talking was okay. But in another mixed school, pupils were in fact practising using them on suitable objects!

I asked Jo why she thought this was the case:

> We work within very different value systems. In the case of the girls' school they seemed to think that information would actually promote under-age or pre-marital sex. We also had to recognise the range of

cultural beliefs within this school and respect these values. Our not being willing to compromise or negotiate around the amount of information given would have led to us not being invited to do any work at all within this school. In these cases, we have to trust that a little information is not a dangerous thing.

I was interested in Jo's statement about her service being driven by 'different values'. What are these values?

That's a good question! It's an interesting journey that led the health promotion service to have a strong value base. I think it's to do with how much we were challenged and how much we had to change when we became involved in training and education around HIV/AIDS. If nothing else, the work around these issues was very much user-led. The forerunners in this work were gay men who in a sense demanded that we consider our sterile, heterosexual and 'safe for us' sex education. This required us to look at our values in depth. Not just values around sex either but about discrimination, prejudice and media exploitation. On top of this, we had the political agenda of 'public health risk' in relation to HIV/AIDS. It felt like we were set the task of education very clearly from two major stakeholders. I believe our values changed somewhat from the medical-led one to a much more aware sociological and societal perspective. All of this has led us to want to educate and inform young people about the real world, with the real choices they have to make. We want them to have the best opportunity to make the best informed choices for themselves around their health and sexuality. And we want to promote this without prejudice.

What other difficulties have you come up against in relation to working with different value systems?

We were recently asked to do work in a boys' day school around sexuality and health. We negotiated with the headmaster about the content of the sessions and felt we had an appropriate plan of work. However, what we hadn't discussed with the headmaster was the ethos of the school and therefore found that some of the content, but more the ways in which we worked, was totally out of kilter with what the young men were used to. For example, they had been given an extremely traditional stereotyped view of masculinity and were all referred to as 'young gentlemen'. They were totally untested and untrained in dealing with feelings and also, interestingly, were so used to rules, traditions, conventions, they were also totally unprepared for even simple decision making. There was mass havoc when the group were asked to make a decision!

What do you think you could have done differently to prevent or help this situation?

I think what it's taught me is that although it is honourable and laudable to have my own and my service's value systems, we must be flexible enough to enable us to provide a service across different cultures and different environments but somehow not lose sight of our own baseline of acceptibility within that.

Interview by Val Williams
Barnardo's

32

Accused

Glyn (not his real name) was a residential social worker for 15 years before moving into a training role in his agency. He is an 'out' gay man who now works within different forums both in and outside his work setting to promote equal opportunities in relation to gay and lesbian issues. Glyn's journey to being comfortable with being 'out' has been a long and painful one and has included some particularly difficult and, he considers, personally dangerous situations to overcome in the workplace.

I asked Glyn to talk about being accused, and what his and others' responses had been to this.

The first time was very early on in my career as a care worker. I was well aware by this point that I was gay, but was still keeping it hidden from family, most friends and particularly from colleagues and management at work. Remember this is approximately 20 years ago now and there hadn't been the publicity, both good and negative, around gay issues.

I had been a care worker in this residential home for young people only about three months when a totally unprecedented event led to the boss finding out I was gay. I was very clear at this stage that no one should know about my sexuality and made sure I gave nothing away. However, one day the whole unit went on an outing bar one kid who ran away into the school grounds and refused to come. Well, in those days, most residential staff 'lived in' and I had a room which I always carefully locked and kept private. Unfortunately, on this occasion this young lad who'd been left behind broke back into the home through the window into my room. He found some magazines in my room which were for gay men and were sexually explicit. He got caught, of course, and he used the magazines to deflect from his own problem. I just couldn't believe it. I thought that would be it, my career as a social worker completely out the window.

To my utter surprise, however, the officer-in-charge handled the situation extremely sympathetically. He told the lad that I had in fact confiscated the magazines from the shed at the bottom of the garden (a usual place for illicit things to be found!) and that I was keeping them locked in my room for safety! He also was not heavy with me, or prejudiced, or punishing. All he said to me was that he was extremely pleased with my work on the unit and had no reason to believe I was anything other than a credit to the staff team.

Although the outcome was positive, I can't tell you about the depth of vulnerability and uncertainty I experienced. You've got to remember that being gay is often seen as the same as being perverted and I was just waiting for that accusation . . .

Although it happened, I didn't have too long to wait for that either. Some years later, when I was a bit further along with the ownership of my sexuality, I was in a houseshare with other gay men. This was proving a positive experience and we were mutually supportive of each other in a caring way. The last room in the house went to a very young man who, I now realise in retrospect, I related to as a client. This I can see was partly because I could not use the fact that I was gay in a positive way at work. I couldn't, for example, empathise or sympathise with young men who I could see were struggling with their sexuality, for fear of my own exposure and possible accusations of promoting sexuality or even of being seductive. However, this young man joined the houseshare and it was obvious from the start he was very troubled and angry. The houseshare didn't really work out for him and he left, still very much troubled and angry in a kind of directionless way. After about a week he phoned and asked to borrow a tenner. I felt for him and also thought, well, ten quid's not much so I sent it to him. A week or two later he phoned again, this time asking for a hundred quid. I was flabbergasted. I couldn't possibly lend him that amount, neither did I want to! I told him I wouldn't and he immediately threatened to phone my work and tell them I was gay.

I was really scared, but I suppose I didn't really think he would. But he began to phone me up at work, with his accusations getting more and more fantastical. He also began to threaten he would phone *The Sun* and tell them about me. What was extremely hard was that his accusations had some truth and some lies in them. I was in fact gay and involved in the gay scene but I was not in any way seductive of the young men I worked with, nor had I ever been anywhere within a hundred miles of having a sexual relationship with anyone I worked with. I've got the same boundaries as any other care worker. You just don't do that kind of thing, whether you're gay or not. The other dreadful thing was that my agency was dealing at the time with a real example of abuse by a member of staff in one of their other children's homes and I was terrified that the accusation made about me would somehow get tied up with this other real situation.

I had to make a decision, and quickly, about what to do about this. I was still deliberating the best strategy and finding it hard to resist my terror, which made me begin to feel that I was in fact guilty of something, when I had a telephone message at work from a reporter from *The Sun*. I telephoned back, just to check the number, hoping desperately that it was a hoax, or it was even this young man himself, but no, it actually was *The Sun* newspaper. That was it, I had to do something.

I went immediately to my boss, and again I was amazed at the speed and sensitivity of the response. The fact that I was gay was not seen as the issue, rather it was the accusation and its effect on me. I also phoned the gay help switchboard and they advised that I would have to get the phone calls taped. This was the only way the police would be able to help. They also advised that I contacted my work's press and publicity department, just in case the story did get out.

My managers agreed to a recording unit being attached to the main office telephone and it was agreed they would support me in taking the accuser to court if necessary. This all happened very quickly and very efficiently. So much so that when the young man phoned again I was primed. When he started the usual stuff I immediately told him that the police had been contacted and the call was being recorded. He immediately hung up. We waited with bated breath for him to ring again, or indeed for the reporter to ring again. Neither happened. Slowly, over the days and then weeks I began to think he wouldn't ring again, and indeed he never did. The crisis was over, everyone gave a sigh of relief and got back on with their work. That was apart from me. Of course, I did feel relief but the impact was enormous: on my self-confidence, on my feelings about being okay about being gay, about the huge risks I felt I took with being a residential social worker. I also felt, in time, a little cynical about the magnanimity of my managers in being able to support me. I began to question just who it was they had been protecting. I also began to see that it was okay me being gay because they liked me. I didn't fit their stereotype. I liked football, I could tell jokes. I kept my gayness in place and didn't threaten anyone with it. My cynicism increased when I saw a lesbian worker being treated really quite badly when she didn't fit in. I began to challenge whether the positive response I had got was anything at all about what I wanted it to be, which was acceptance of my sexuality.

This rather cynical view has been reinforced in the few years since this dramatic incident. A bit after this very bad time I got involved in gay and lesbian issues in the agency and helped set up a support service. My name was on a poster advertising this service and one of the kids saw it. This got back to his parents and they asked one of my colleagues. This staff member just presumed the parents knew and talked freely to them about me being gay. They hadn't in fact known, and had just been digging for information. This led to another round of uproar but in a quieter, more insidious way. By then, staff at least had been 'educated' to some extent, through training in HIV/AIDS, so they were on the surface very supportive of gay issues. However, the children and young people had no such cares and they had no qualms about abusing me about my sexuality. This led to verbal abuse, having salt thrown all over me and having quite serious damage done to my car. That was when I realised that colleague support was a bit less than I hoped. They were good enough at responding to crisis but not so able to respond to the day-to-day abuse and discrimination. They tend to laugh it off or not take it all that seriously. For me it does feel serious, and something I face every day.

In terms of a positive end to this story I do find in a training environment people are beginning to hear the message about it being hard to be male and in a residential care setting, but even harder to be male and gay in a residential care setting. Also, I did have a good experience earlier this year. I was in a gay bar in Brighton and in walked a young man I had worked with years ago. He had finally come to terms with his sexuality and although it had never been discussed between us, or even mentioned all those years ago, he was able to say that he'd always felt supported by me. That was good. That made me feel good.

Interview by Val Williams

33
Use of Physical Restraint in Children's Residential Care

Her Paul Clarke explores some of the issues raised by the use of physical restraint for those working with young people.

> A semi-circle of little boys, their bodies streaked with coloured clay, sharp sticks in their hands, were standing on the beach making no noise at all.
> 'Fun and games,' said the officer.

> William Golding, *Lord of the Flies*

One of the most controversial elements of the use of power in residential child care is the application of physical restraint. It is an area in which staff can feel immobilised by indecision, a circumstance which has been partly brought about by the lack of clarity given by the attendant policy and guidance. Accordingly few agencies have demonstrated a commitment to delivering and developing appropriate staff training methods. None of the Diploma in Social Work courses approved under the Residential Child Care Initiative (a training project which was set up following *The Review of Residential Child Care*: Utting, 1991) provide training in the direct use of physical restraint, and fewer than 30% of the local authorities who responded to a survey have active training programmes in operation. This is in spite of the fact that the need for training in this area of work has been identified by the numerous reviews and inquiries that have looked into standards of practice in residential child care. Recommendation 76 of *Choosing with Care*, the Report of the Committee of Inquiry into the Selection, Development and Management of Staff in Children's Homes (Committee of Inquiry, 1992), states that 'The Government should issue full guidance for staff on the issues of control, restraint and physical contact with children in residential care, keep this up to date, and reinforce it by ensuring the provision of authoritative training material that allows staff to apply the guidance in real situations.'

Many commentators felt that the subsequent *Guidance on Permissible Forms of Control in Children's Residential Care*

(Department of Health, 1993) fell short of this recommendation and also served to further cloud the issue by asking authorities to use their discretion in deciding whether or not to train staff in the use of physical restraint: 'They should make a judgement about the need for training for staff working in open accommodation' (para 11.1).

● Requests for a clearer policy have also come from various groups, many of whom have demanded action following particular incidents. Jean Cape (1996), a residential care manager, commented in a letter to *Community Care*: 'We are creating an environment where young people are out of control, have a free hand to do what they want, cause damage and destruction, abuse staff and other residents . . . we feel powerless to stop them.' Similarly the public service union, Unison, have said in a newspaper article: 'Violence is escalating in children's homes with violent young people all too often being allowed to return to units where they have already attacked staff' (*Bristol Evening Post*, December 1995). ●

Residential care nowadays is mainly populated by adolescents (largely in the 14–17 age range) who are more likely to have suffered numerous foster care breakdowns before reaching the 'residential' end of the care continuum. One may assume therefore that residential care houses older children whose problems have become protracted. As Berridge (1985) points out in his study of residential child care, 'to dispose of a few cherished illusions . . . those expecting to find the children's home sheltering a group of sad, young orphans aching for a loving bosom . . . are more likely to find older adolescents, who can be extremely awkward and anti-social.' Not surprisingly, the application of physical restraint in residential child care is not a 'risk-free' area. At the time of writing, there is at least one authority that awaits the outcome of a court hearing (and possible claims for compensation).

The fear of litigation is matched by the shock within the profession which followed the Pindown Inquiry (Levy and Kahan, 1991) where abusive regimes of control were found to have been imposed on young people in residential care. Thus the agencies who provide residential child care respond to the training needs of staff (with regard to the application of physical restraint) with caution. Coupled with this, many practitioners themselves have voiced concerns about the application of physical restraint. One of the main reasons given by staff is the requirements of the Children Act 1989 Volume 4 Guidance and Regulations relating to residential care, which correctly stresses the importance of informing children and young people who are being 'looked after' of their right to make 'representations' (complaints).

Research findings suggest that staff in crisis situations feel constrained in applying physical restraint, fearing that hostile young people have nothing to lose in making an unjustified complaint against them. They also fear that the 'procedural' nature of a 'representation' may lead them to be the subject of disciplinary action. Many comment that even unsubstantiated and invalid complaints can create a 'no smoke without fire' situation, in which they have no right of redress. This view is supported by the findings of *Choosing with Care* (Committee of Inquiry, 1992), which reported that 'on many occasions we were informed of situations where staff have been forced to defend themselves against attack by a young person and, having done so, found that the child has made a complaint against them. As a result, staff have become wary of using any form of physical restraint and feel unable to attempt to restrain children who are behaving violently.' A climate of passivity and indecision (with regard to clear directions for practice) seems to persist, despite clarion calls for action from many respected commentators. As long ago as 1981 the Dartington Research Unit pointed to the importance of appropriate forms of staff training in methods of control (Millham et al., 1981), and more recently Allan Levy (1994) in an article on the subject of restraint training says: 'It is very dangerous when practice is fragmented and there is no approved method which is implemented consistently. If children are going to be restrained it is better that the people doing it know what they are doing.'

With regard to practice in this area of work, few studies have been subject to legitimate, systematic, published or comparative research. Predetermined plans of action based on acquired skills learned from training courses are rarely used in residential settings (other than those used in certain custodial or secure institutions). Good practice is directed by clear policies which emphasise the importance of good personal relationships with young people, but which also accept that staff may on occasion have to restrain children in order to prevent them injuring themselves or others. This is true as much for parents in the domestic setting as it is for staff in the children's home. However staff in children's homes lack the emotional, economic and other sanctions that a parent has with their own child. They therefore need to draw on their own professional skills and expertise. Section V of the Department of Health's *Guidance on Permissible Forms of Control in Children's Residential Care* (1993) states: 'The proper use of physical restraint requires skill and judgement, as well as knowledge of non-harmful methods of restraint.' It goes on to recommend: 'any in-service training on the use of techniques of physical restraint must only be given as part of a programme which puts its use within the full context of care and control in residential child care.'

This context includes the following key areas:

1   the structure of the living environment;
2   the suitability of placement;
3   the outcome of aggressive or violent behaviour.

The structure of the living environment

Attention to the 'living environment' should include attempts to eliminate the worst excesses of institutional living (Kahan, 1994). Restrictions placed on individual choice (as seen in food preferences, leisure activities, television/video likes and dislikes) are likely to provoke an angry response in the most mild mannered adolescent. Also of importance is the need for privacy (for example, a room of their own) and security. Residential care can be an imposing place. Where any collective of adolescents are housed, you would not be surprised to discover that bullying may be commonplace and structures should therefore be in place which attempt to eradicate this.

The suitability of placement

Care and control management also includes the identification of those children and young people who may be in need of firmer areas of control. 'Statements of purpose', as defined by the Children Act 1989, are intended to ensure that young people are appropriately placed in a unit where both the skills and expertise of the staff and the available resources match a young person's individual needs. The 1991 Review of Children's Homes in Wales, *Accommodating Children* (HMSO, 1991), made as its major recommendation the need for two types of children's homes, with 'children who are displaying challenging behaviour' being placed in homes separate from children who are in residential care 'as a result of circumstances rather than behaviour'. The Children Act 1989 stresses that homes have to 'work with children to prepare for a definite goal', for example by 'addressing a child's unacceptable behaviour by means of a systematic behavioural regime'. Needless to say the Act also says that staff working in these units need to be appropriately trained.

Sadly many commentators report that 'statements of purpose' are not being adhered to, possibly as a result of public spending cuts which have reduced the numbers of staff and residential units. The Warner Report *Choosing with Care* (Committee of Inquiry, 1992) noted a 20% drop in numbers of residential units in England since 1989. This has created a scarcity of available beds and therefore inappropriate placements continue to be commonplace.

The outcome of aggressive or violent behaviour

Another essential element in control management is the requirement that all staff and young people are clear about the outcome of aggressive or violent behaviour. This should be based upon an agreed policy that directs staff action during the initial intervention and that determines the rebuke or reprimand. (Obviously responses may differ according to severity or context but there should be some general consensus as to what the range of likely responses will be.) Young people may expect, indeed demand, carers to set boundaries on their behaviour.

In conclusion, there can be no doubt that staff training in the use of physical restraint, that is subject to official approval and direction, is long overdue.

However, control management remains an essential skill within children's residential care. Physical restraint should never be used to enforce regimes of discipline on young people, but it should not come as a surprise to staff that caring for adolescents occasionally requires them to provide a safe living environment for young people through the demonstration of competent authority and leadership.

References

Berridge, D. (1985) *Children's Homes*, Oxford: Basil Blackwell.
Cape, J. (1996) 'Lip service paid to child care plans', *Community Care*, January.
Committee of Inquiry (1992) *Choosing with Care*, Report of the Committee of Inquiry into the Selection, Development and Management of Staff in Children's Homes, London: HMSO.
Department of Health (1993) *Guidance on Permissible Forms of Control in Children's Residential Care*, London: HMSO.
HMSO (1991) *Accommodating Children*, Review of Children's Homes in Wales, London: HMSO.
Kahan, B. (1994) *Growing up in Groups*, London: HMSO.
Levy, A. (1994) Quoted in *Community Care*, 7–13 July.

Levy, A. and Kahan, B. (1991) *The Pindown Experience and the Protection of Children*, Report of the Staffordshire Child Care Inquiry, Stafford: Staffordshire County Council.

Millham, S., Bullock, R., Hosie, K. and Haak, M. (1981) *Issues of Control in Residential Child Care*, Dartington: Dartington Social Research Project, DHSS.

Utting, Sir William (1991) *The Review of Residential Child Care*, London: HMSO.

Paul Clarke
Senior Training Officer
Bath and North East Somerset Council

Index

164   *Index*